# French Art

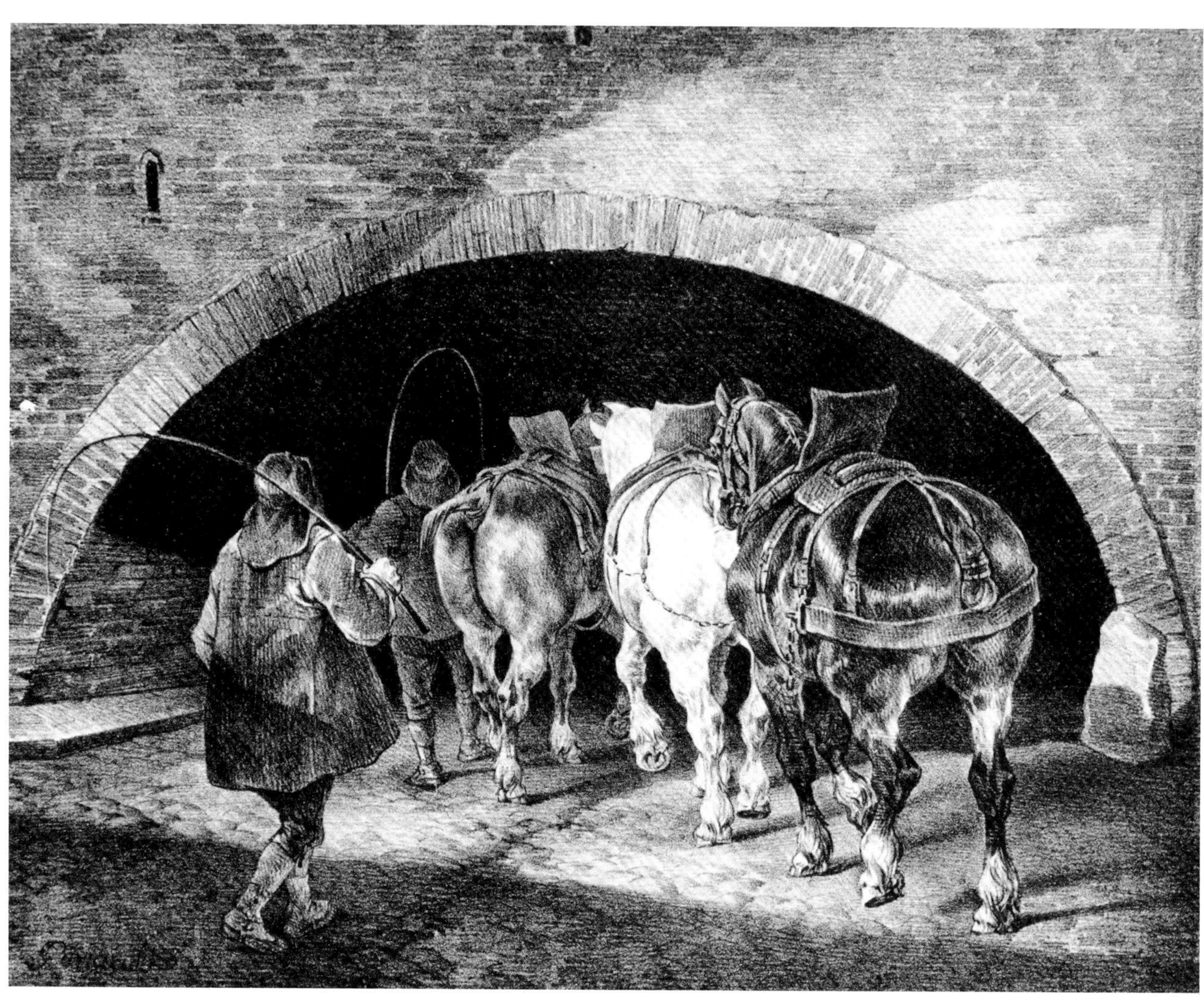

Jean Louis Théodore Géricault (1791-1824)
*Entrance to the Adelphi Wharf*, 1821
Lithograph, 2nd state, 12½ x 15¹³⁄₁₆″
Museum purchase
1965.51

# French Art

MEAD ART MUSEUM MONOGRAPHS
VOLUMES 8 & 9    WINTER 1987–1988

EDITED BY FRANK TRAPP

MEAD ART MUSEUM, AMHERST COLLEGE
AMHERST, MASSACHUSETTS 01002

Production: Chameleon Books
Designer: Arnold Skolnick
Design Assistant: Nancy Crompton
Photography: Frank Ward, David Stansbury
Editor: David Frankel
Editorial Assistant: Ellen Dibble
Typography: MGL Graphics, N.Y.
Printing and Binding: Studley Press, MA.



This Monograph has been published with funds
provided by The Associates of Fine Arts at Amherst.

ISBN 0-914337-10-6

# CONTENTS


Introduction and Acknowledgments
FRANK TRAPP
6

Painting in Eighteenth-Century France
ERIC M. ZAFRAN
8

Other French Masterworks and Their Artists
FRANK TRAPP AND JUDITH A. BARTER
20

Nineteenth-Century French Prints
From the Collection of Edward C. Crossett
JAY M. FISHER
48

Incunabula of Lithography in France
FRANK TRAPP
55

# Introduction

**FRANK TRAPP**

The art of France is well represented in the Mead Art Museum, and it is the purpose of the present publication to give some idea of the character of that aspect of the Amherst College Collection. For the most part, French sculptures at Mead are reviewed in volume IV of the present series of monographs, the 1983 issue, which is devoted to European sculpture. Some notable samples of French accomplishment during the medieval period will be considered on some future occasion. For present purposes we shall concentrate on the art of painting from the Baroque period onward. A small but distinguished group of paintings representative of the Rococo developments of the eighteenth century forms the focus of an essay contributed by a guest author, Eric M. Zafran, curator of Renaissance and Baroque art at the Walters Art Gallery, Baltimore. A more extensive series of works from the Baroque and later periods will also be surveyed as a kind of anthology. While much remains to be done in expanding these aspects of our representation of the French heritage in the visual arts, the quality and variety of the objects already available in the permanent collection is reassuring in its suggestion that such a purpose may now be realistically proposed as a further collecting goal for the Museum.

By happy chance from this point of view, the tastes of William Crossett, whose personal collection forms the cornerstone of our holdings in the graphic arts, were well disposed toward the printmakers of France. Thus we are able to present the remarkable contribution of the early French master Jacques Callot (1592–1635), for example, with original impressions of superb quality. Crossett's interests as a collector showed considerable historical range, however. In the area of French art he exhibited a particular preference for the contribution of French printmakers of the nineteenth century. Accordingly, another essay prepared for the present volume by Jay Fisher, curator of prints and drawings at the Baltimore Museum of Art, will be devoted to that aspect of the Crossett Collection.

In recognition of the great value of the print collection in expanding our capacity to represent the artistic developments of many lands, it has long been our practice at Mead to acquire prints that complement the contents of the original Crossett bequest. It has, for instance, been possible over the years to assemble a range of the so-called "incunabula" of lithography—works produced in the early nineteenth century, immediately following Aloys Senefelder's invention of that widely adopted medium. Although lithography soon attracted many artists, it was in France that the novelties of lithography were most eagerly exploited. Building upon the foundations laid by Crossett in his acquisition of a few masterpieces of French lithography (among them several superb sheets by Eugène Delacroix, and a fine Paul Cézanne *Bathers*), a representative body of works in that medium were subsequently either purchased for the collection or attracted as gifts. Whether by bequest, gift, or purchase, the historical purview of the collection now includes fine works by such French masters of the early modern period as Odilon Redon, Henri de Toulouse-Lautrec, Georges Rouault, and Henri Matisse. Aspects of that further side of the print collection must await discussion on another occasion, but the incunabula of lithography constitute a self-standing topic which also recommended itself for inclusion in the present monograph.

Given these still-accumulating resources, it is by now possible to represent a considerable variety of the artistic developments in France, if not by any means the whole of its enormous range.

As befits a proper study collection, there are, of course, many themes to be discerned within the reserves of French art at Mead. Revealing comparisons with the contemporaneous expression of other national schools are but one of many instructive possibilities that come to mind. And particularly with the quickening pace of artistic exchanges during the more modern periods, a wealth of interpretive insights is invited, as our capacity to substantiate those cross-cultural patterns grows.

## ACKNOWLEDGMENTS

It is always a pleasure to thank our guest authors for their generosity in taking time from other, more immediate obligations to give our readers the benefit of their special expertise. Deep appreciation should be expressed to the High Museum for making available the color separations used in preparing the present publication. And those closer to home will, I trust, appreciate the warm respect with which their contributions to these publications are viewed.

Frank Trapp

# Painting in Eighteenth-Century France

## ERIC M. ZAFRAN

Although our image of painting in eighteenth-century France is one of great freedom and brio, the fact is that the artistic life of the period was quite rigid. It was dominated by the Académie Royal de Peinture et Sculpture. An aspiring young artist first entered the studio of an established academician for several years of training in the fundamentals of art. He could then be admitted to the Academy on a probational status (as an *agréé*) and could compete for the coveted Prix de Rome, which, if he won it, would support an extended period of study in Rome. Ultimately he had to submit a specified *morceau de réception* in order to be *réçu*, or received, as a full member of the academy. Only the members of the Academy had the privilege of receiving royal commissions and showing their works at the official exhibitions known as the Salon.

Equally codified was the approach to subject matter. According to a hierarchy of genres in effect since the seventeenth century,[1] the most elevated subject was history painting. This *grand genre*, as it was known, included sacred and ancient history as well as mythology and allegory. It was the element of imagination necessary in creating these compositions that placed them above those dependent on direct observation, which, ranked according to their importance, were portraiture, still life, and landscape. The collection of French eighteenth-century paintings at Amherst, although small, encompasses works by artists of the Academy who achieved prominence in each of these categories.

The first painting to be considered is the *Allegorical Female Figure* (fig. 1)[2] by Jean-Baptiste-Marie Pierre (1714–89). Pierre, who was born in Paris, first studied with Charles Joseph Natoire, and in 1734 won the *Prix de Rome*, which allowed him to spend five years at the Académie Française in Rome. There, as was the tradition, he copied the great works of the Renaissance; the influence of Michelangelo in particular continued to be important to him, and is even evident in the sculptural forms within this painting. Upon his return to France, Pierre began exhibiting at the Salon and made his reputation as a painter of heroic mythological and religious subjects as well as with an occasional decorative project. He received his first commission from the royal family in 1747, and through his dedication, wealth, and obsequious personality advanced through the ranks of the Académie Royale, so that

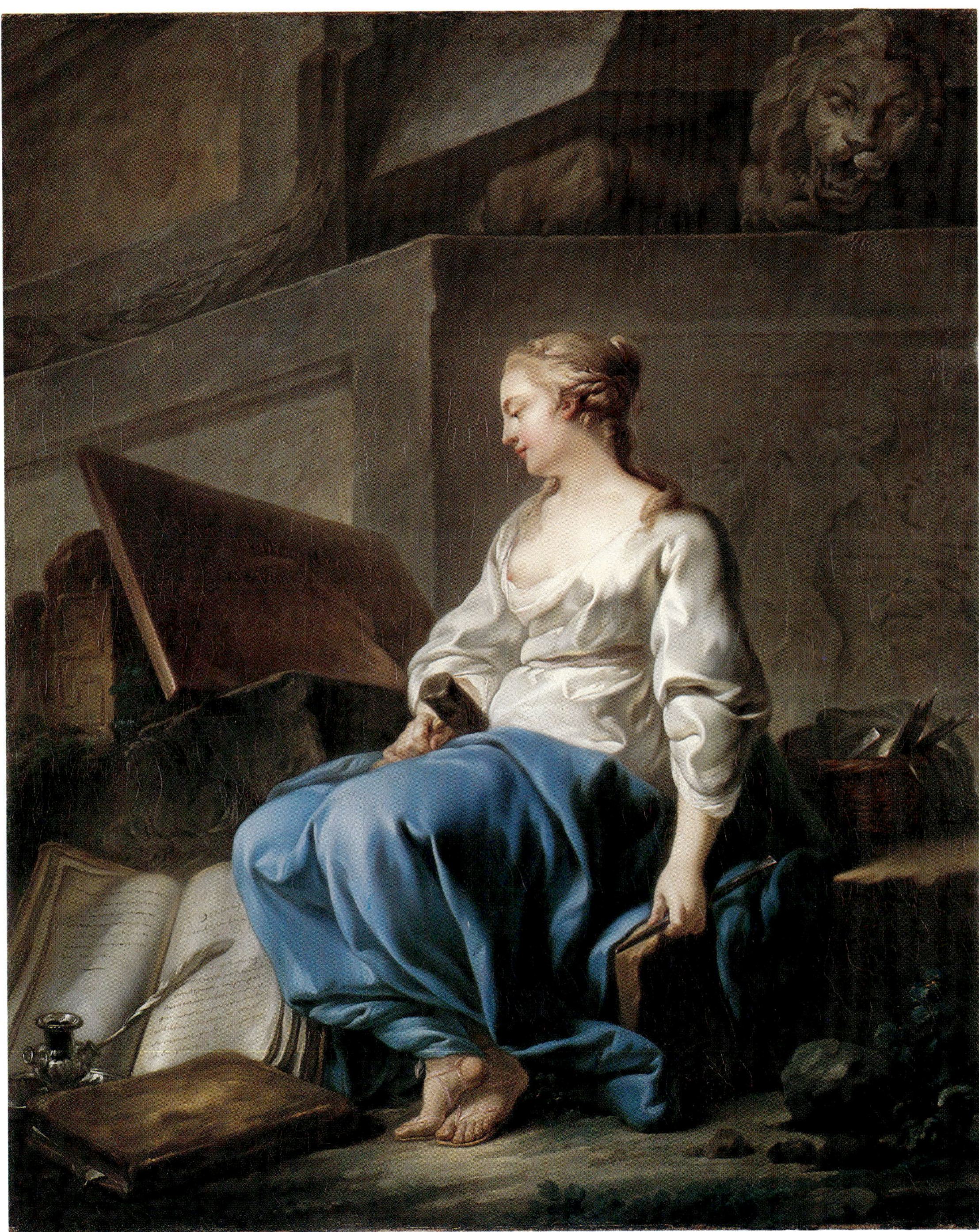

Fig. 11

Jean-Baptiste-Marie Pierre (1714–89)
*Allegorical Female Figure (Allegory of Sculpture?)*
Oil on canvas, 35 ¾ x 28 ¾ ″
Museum purchase
1978.35

following the death of François Boucher, in 1770, he was appointed *Premier Peintre du Roi* and, in 1778, director of the Academy. Once having achieved these powerful positions, however, he painted less and less.

Pierre depicted allegorical female figures on several occasions, and his treatment of such a figure in the Amherst painting is similar in type, pose, and handling to the set of the four Virtues he painted for the Salle du Conseil at Fontainebleau in 1753.[3] The exact subject of this painting, however, is not clear. In the past she has been identified as Sculpture, but no representatives of the other liberal arts with which she would have composed a set have been located.[4] Moreover, though the young woman holds a hammer and chisel, she does not have about her the other traditional attributes of sculpture—such as the compass, crayon, and classical torso—detailed in contemporary iconographic guides.[5] Instead, this lovely figure seems totally absorbed in regarding the inscription she has just engraved into the stone plaque. It says, in Latin, "Heartfelt gratitude is more long-lasting than bronze." The plaque is probably intended for placement on the large sepulchral monument behind her, supported by the ferocious stone lion. The large books and inkwell contribute to the notion that this figure is the allegorical embodiment of a sentiment such as loyalty or remembrance.

As the *Premier Peintre du Roi* and director of the Academy, Pierre could easily use his influence to further the careers of those younger artists whom he favored. One who benefited from this to a great extent was the creator of the next painting to be considered in the history category, Hughes Taraval (1729–85). Taraval was in fact one of the last of the eighteenth-century masters to carry on the tradition of *"la grande décoration,"* before the Revolution put an end to such self-indulgent forms.

Taraval's father, a painter in the employ of the king of Sweden, was his first teacher. Following his father's death, in 1750, the young Taraval returned to Paris. At the age of twenty-one he entered the school of the Academy in the atelier of Pierre, who helped point him toward his future career as a master of large-scale decorative projects. In 1756 he won the Academy's *Grand Prix* for his *Job Reproached by His Wife* (Musée des Arts, Marseilles). He thus was able to enter the École Royale des Élèves Protégés, under the direction of Carle van Loo, and three years later, in 1759, he departed for Rome. There Natoire was the director of the Académie de France, and he encouraged this diligent *pensionnaire.* Taraval's *Venus and Adonis* (National Museum, Stockholm), painted in 1760, shows that he had carefully absorbed the lessons of antiquity, and of Raphael, Domenichino, and Annibale. This painting was subsequently exhibited at the Salon of 1765. Diderot judged the rendering of Venus's nude back "beautiful, very beautiful," and that same year the painter was accepted as an *agréé* by the Academy.

Having returned to Paris in 1763, Taraval, with Pierre's help, had already launched his career as a painter of decorative schemes. He began with works in the residence of the Duc d'Orléans. Then he received a commission for mythological scenes for the bedroom of the royal château of Gustave III, in Stockholm. In 1767 Taraval had his first commission from the French royal family—for overdoors for the château of Bellevue, again of mythological subjects. In 1769, to gain full admittance to the Academy, he exhibited one of his most ambitious works, *The Triumph of Bacchus*, or *Autumn*, for the ceiling of the Gallery of Apollo in the Louvre. Other major commissions included religious subjects such as *The Marriage of Saint Louis*, 1773, for the chapel of the École Royale Militaire. In 1781, Louis XVI commissioned from him two religious subjects for the Chapel of the Trinity at Fontainebleau. In 1783, Taraval was appointed artistic director of the Gobelins tapestry manufactory. In the year of his death he exhibited another major work at the Salon, *The Infant Hercules Strangling the Serpents in His Cradle* (Louvre).

Taraval received one of his most important royal commissions in 1776.[6] It was for a large painting to serve as a design for one of a series of tapestries, by various artists, devoted to "The Loves of the Gods." The project was conceived by the king's *directeur des bâtiments,* Comte d'Angiviller, to help revitalize the standards of history painting. It imitated a project devised by the count's predecessor, the Marquis de Marigny, in 1757. Taraval's choice of subject, *The Triumph of Amphitrite,* was exhibited at the Salon of 1777, and although its dependence on earlier masters was recognized, it was considered a great success.[7] The painting, now in the Louvre, was among those sketched by the painter Gabriel de Saint-Aubin in his copy of the Salon guidebook.[8] Not only was it woven several times as a

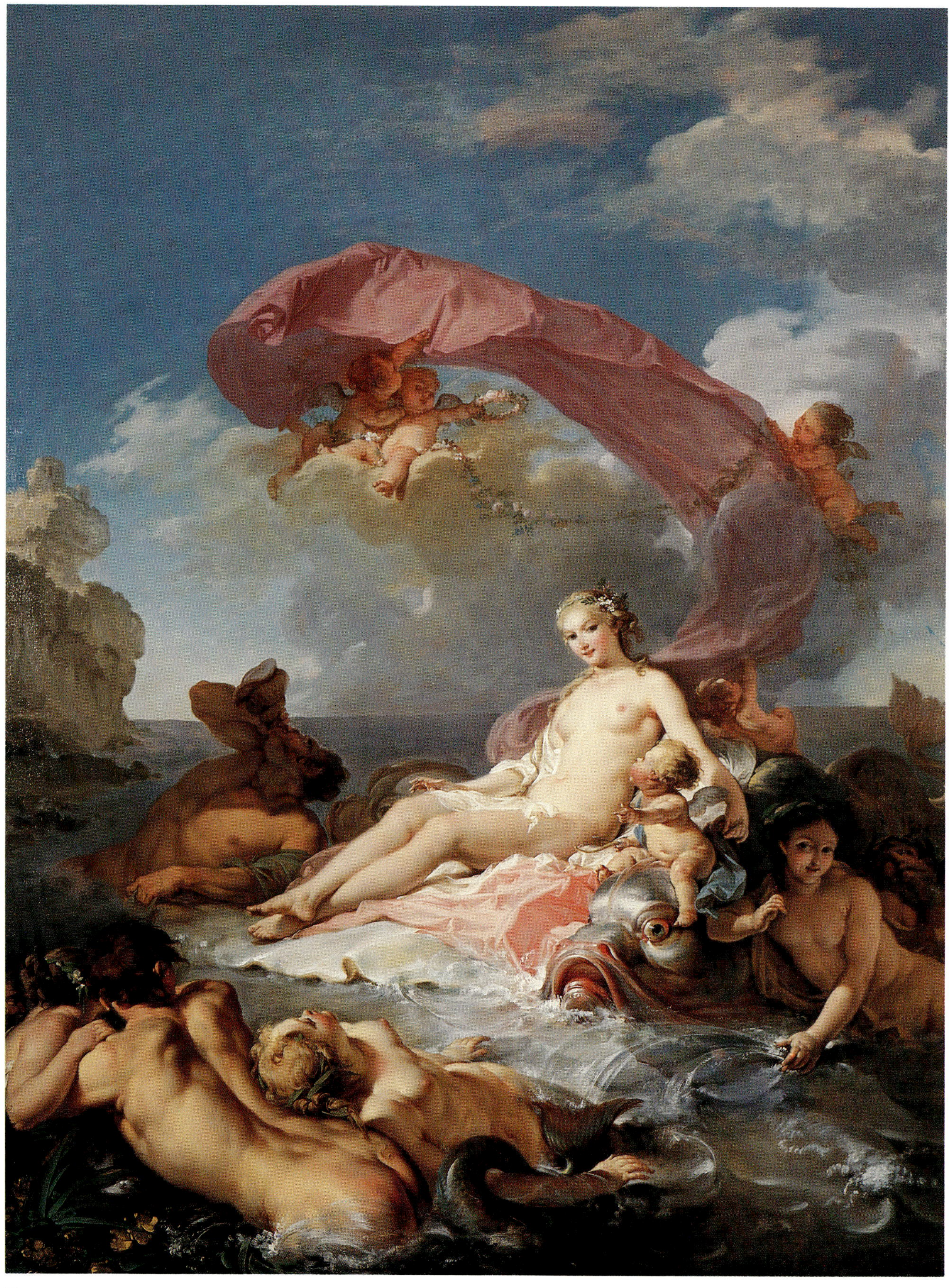

Fig. 2

tapestry, but a number of oil replicas and sketches of it were also produced by Taraval and his atelier.[9] The most important of these was the smaller version that Taraval exhibited with a pendant *Diana Surprised at Her Bath by Actaeon* at the Salon of 1781.

It is this second Salon version by Taraval that is now at Amherst (fig. 2).[10] Although Diderot dismissed the painter's works at the 1781 Salon with a few derogatory remarks,[11] other critics were again full of praise,[12] and Carmontelle, in an anonymous pamphlet, declared that "the effect of the *clair de lune* was marvelous."[13]

The subject of Taraval's painting is derived from Greek mythology. The Nereid Amphitrite is brought from her retreat in the Atlas mountains to be wed with the sea-god Poseidon. She is shown in triumphal procession as queen of the ocean, gliding over the waves on the backs of tritons and dolphins and assisted by Nereids and putti. The theme had previously been treated by the painters Nicolas Coypel and Bon Boullongne. Depictions of other mythological subjects, including Pierre's *Rape of Europa* of 1750,[14] provided compositional elements, but as contemporary critics were aware, it was the work of Boucher that most inspired Taraval. There were in fact many Boucher scenes of sea-borne triumphs available as models, the most important being *The Triumph* or *Birth of Venus* (National Museum, Stockholm). One of the engravings (fig. 3) after Boucher's oval *Birth and Triumph of Venus* of 1743 (now in a private collection in New York) would have been an especially accessible source. The engraving focuses in a similar way on the single central nude supported by sea deities with a silken canopy floating above her.

Taraval's painting would not, however, be mistaken for a work of Boucher. The composition is not as languorous, and the colors, particularly the pinks, are much more intense. As seen in the Amherst replica, which is in a better state of preservation than the earlier Louvre version, Taraval was a master of brilliant tonality, voluptuous forms, and exquisite finish. This gem of a painting sums up all that we think of as implied by the term Rococo.

After history painting, portraiture was the most important category of painting. It held an especial fascination in an era when physiognomies were felt to reveal the true character of an individual. The eighteenth century in France was indeed a great era of por-

Fig. 2

Hughes Taraval (1729–85)
*The Triumph of Amphitrite*, 1780
Oil on canvas, 50¾ x 38¼ "
Museum purchase
1976.2

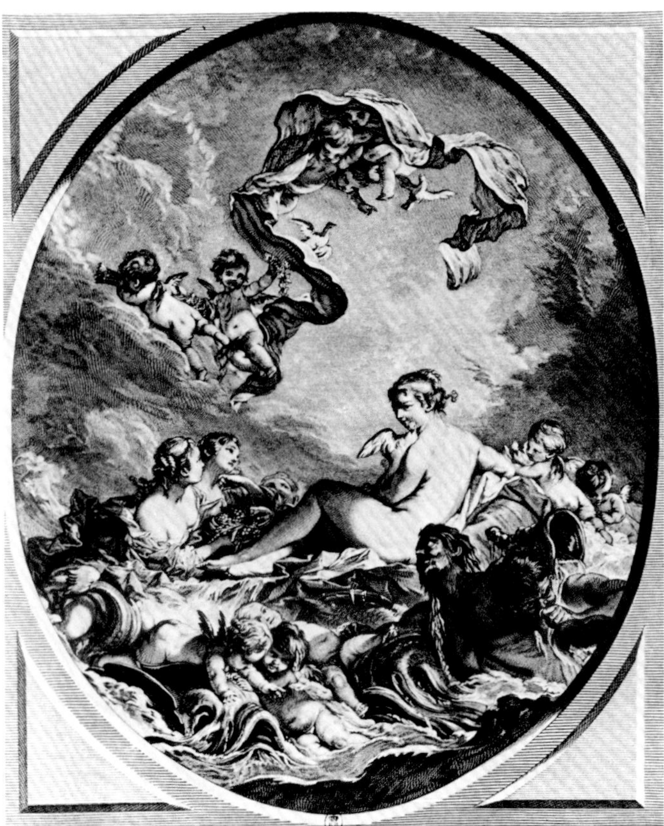

Fig. 3

After François Boucher
*The Birth of Venus*
Engraving

traiture, and one of the greatest specialists was Elisabeth Louise Vigée-Lebrun. Having gained admittance to the Academy by the express command of her patroness, and the frequent subject of her paintings, Marie Antoinette, she exhibited at the Salon of 1783, and a contemporary writer commented, "[Her] paintings are also the most highly praised; they are talked about, they are the topics of conversation at court and in Paris, in suppers, in literary circles. . . .When someone announces that he has just come from the Salon, the first thing he is asked is: Have you seen Madame Lebrun? What do you think of Madame Lebrun? And immediately the answer suggested is: Madame Lebrun, is she not astonishing?"[15] Madame Lebrun's close ties with the royal family made it necessary for her to flee Paris in October 1789, which she did on the public coach for Italy. In that country her aristocratic connections and her talent assured her a continued successful career. She passed through Florence and received a commission for the grand duke's collection of artists' self-portraits at the Uffizi. This she fulfilled after her arrival in Rome that November with a charming *Self-Portrait at an Easel*.[16] In April of 1790 she was elected a member of the Roman Accademia di San Luca, for which she painted a more direct self-portrait.[17] Both of these works were repeatedly copied, and the *Self-Portrait* at Amherst (fig. 4)[18] is a copy of the Accademia painting. It still manages to convey the directness of character and the flair for style in dress and pose that distinguish Vigée-Lebrun's work.

Of the remaining genres of painting, the Mead Art Museum has outstanding examples of both still life and landscape. Of the two categories, the still life is perhaps the most mysterious; here, through the skill of the painter, ordinary objects, flowers, or fruit are given a monumental presence and transformed into permanent images of timeless beauty. While Chardin may be the artist we most readily think of in this context, one of the greatest of still-life painters from the first half of the eighteenth century was Alexandre-François Desportes (1661–1743), who is represented in the Mead collection by *Still Life with Dead Birds and Fruit* (fig. 5).[19]

Desportes learned the Flemish tradition of still-life painting from his first teacher, Nicasius Bernaert. Following that master's death, he worked with Claude Audran III on various decorative projects in which he painted the animals. For a period of two years in the

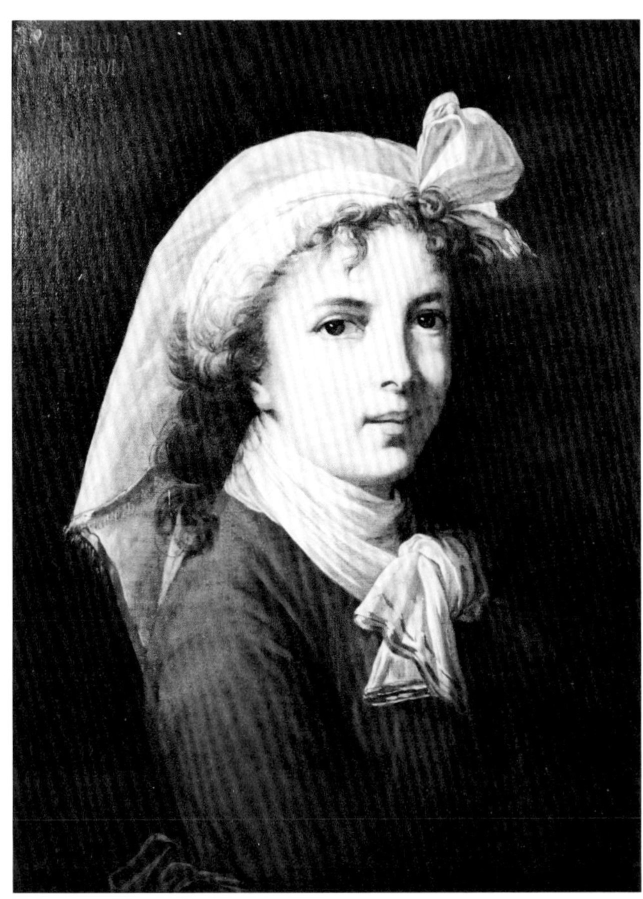

Fig. 4

Marie-Louise-Elisabeth Vigée-Lebrun (1755–1842),
  Copy after
*Self-Portrait of the Artist*
Oil on canvas, 23 ¼ x 16 ⅝'
Gift of Charles K. Arter, '36
1961.9

mid 1690s, the artist was called to Warsaw to work for King Sobieski as a portraitist, recording the king and queen and members of the Polish court.

In 1699, shortly after his return to Paris, Desportes was *reçu* by the academy as a painter of animals with his *Self-Portrait as a Hunter Accompanied by His Dogs* (Louvre). This work became well known, and was the basis for a number of commissioned portraits, but it was as a painter of still lifes, animals, and the hunt that Desportes gained his greatest fame. His first royal commission for such subjects came in 1700, when he painted scenes of hunting for the Ménagerie at Versailles. Recognizing his skill, Louis XIV gave him a pension and a residence in the Louvre. The painter produced many additional hunting scenes as well as portraits of the king's favorite dogs.

In 1712, Desportes was allowed to go to England in the retinue of the French ambassador, the Duc d'Aumont. He remained six months, executing many works for the English nobility. Returning to France, he painted additional hunt and still-life decorations at both Versailles and Marly. During the Regency, he worked for

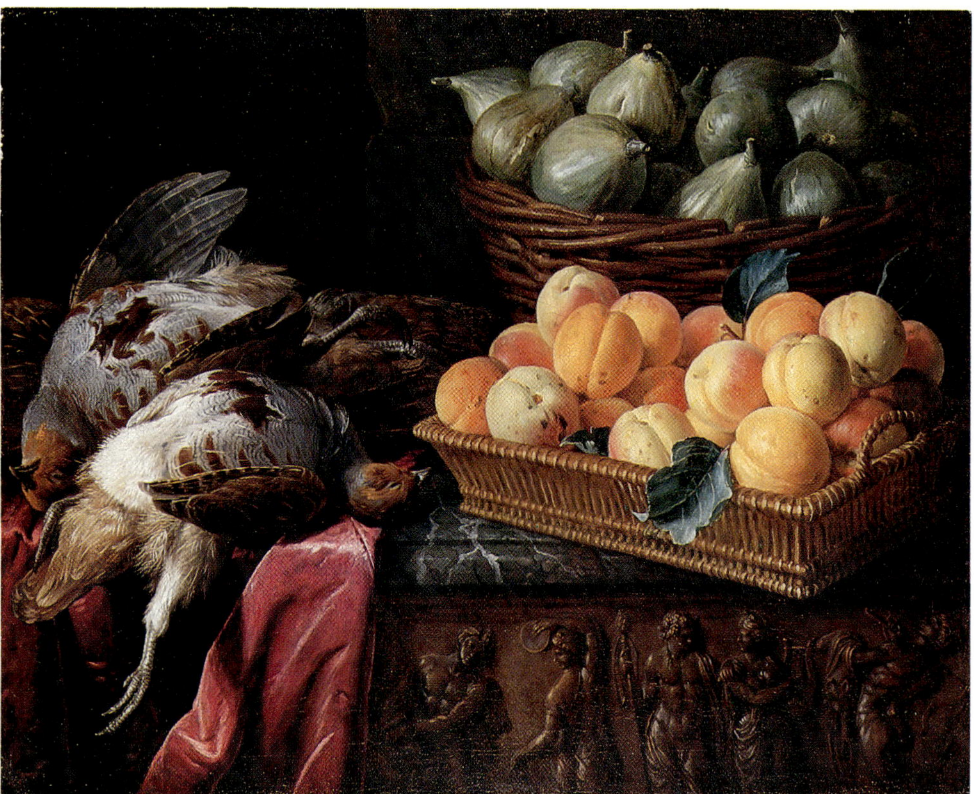

Fig. 5

Fig. 5

Alexandre-François Desportes (1661–1743)
*Still Life with Dead Birds and Fruit*, 1739
Oil on canvas, 18½ x 22″
Museum purchase
1978.34


Fig. 6

Jean-Baptiste Legillon (1739–97)
*Interior of a Ruined Barn*, 1789
Musée du Louvre, Paris

the Duc d'Orléans at the Palais Royal, and decorated many other châteaux. He became a favorite of Louis XV, whom he accompanied on the hunt and whose dogs he also painted. Desportes exhibited regularly at the Salon and was as popular as he was prolific. The biographer d'Argenville noted, "There was hardly a house of any significance which did not possess one of his works—be it a portrait, animals, hunting scene, overdoor, or buffet."[20] D'Argenville also called attention to the remarkable oil sketches on paper that Desportes did as preparatory studies. These works, recently unearthed at the library of Sèvres, attest to his impassioned observation of all of nature's phenomena—clouds, plants, and animals.[21]

This small still life, which clearly shows the artist's mastery of varied textures, from the downy softness of the birds' feathers to the smooth surface of the marble table top and the pitted skins of the peaches, is one of a number of similar still lifes from the mid and late 1730s.[22] The classicizing relief on the table edge is also

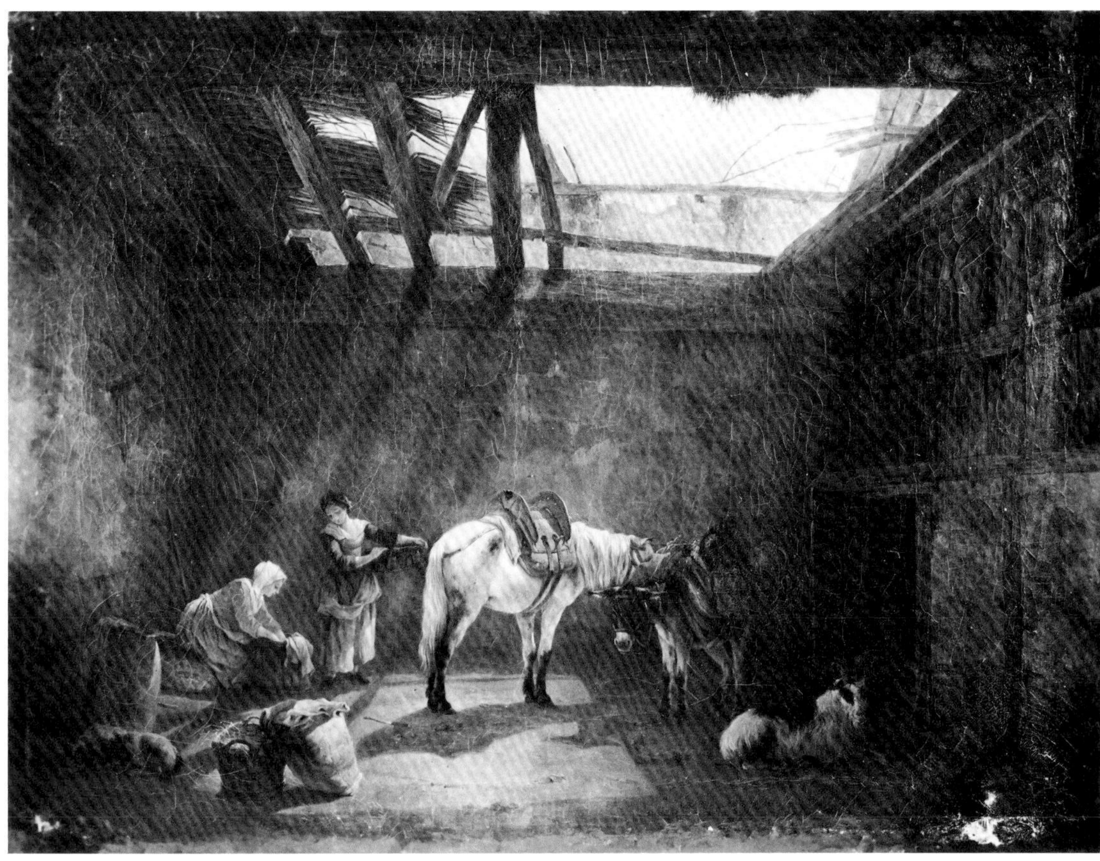

Fig. 6

of a kind that appears in other of Desportes's still lifes and may be based on a work by the Flemish sculptor François du Quesnoy.[23] These figures of pagan celebrants add a joyous note of richness to this modern display of sacrificial goods.

The work representing the category of landscape painting in the Amherst Collection is actually by an artist of Flemish origin, Jean-Baptiste Legillon (1739–97).[24] Born and trained in Bruges, he went in 1760 to Rouen, where the local *académie* was under the direction of Jean-Baptiste Descamps. Two years later, having attained the *académie*'s first prize, he returned home, but soon he began a number of trips back to France, spending time not only in Rouen but also in Paris, Marseilles, and Toulouse. Then, like so many French artists, he went south to Italy, where he lived primarily in Rome from late in 1770 to 1774. According to early sources, Legillon executed only drawings and watercolors in this period, and did not take up oil painting until 1776. The painter settled in Paris

and entered the Académie Royale, exhibiting at the Salon of 1789 his *morceau de réception*, *Interior of a Ruined Barn* (fig. 6), now in the Louvre.[25] The painting at Amherst (fig. 7)[26] is dated two years earlier and both works reveal the same careful attention to detail. A sheet of goat studies from 1786 (fig. 8)[27] by Legillon, in the Boymans-van Beuningen Museum, is quite possibly done in preparation for the rather humorous creature that appears in the Amherst painting. What most impresses us about the painting, however, is the glowing light. This very Italianate quality shows not only the impact of the artist's own voyage, but the lingering influence of such seventeenth-century masters as Aelbert Cuyp and Adam Pynacker.

Legillon exhibited again at the Salon of 1791, and died in Paris in 1797. Only a small number of his works survive,[28] and the Amherst painting is notable, since it reveals him as a painter of great sensitivity and shows the achievements that even a seemingly minor master was capable of in this great era of art.

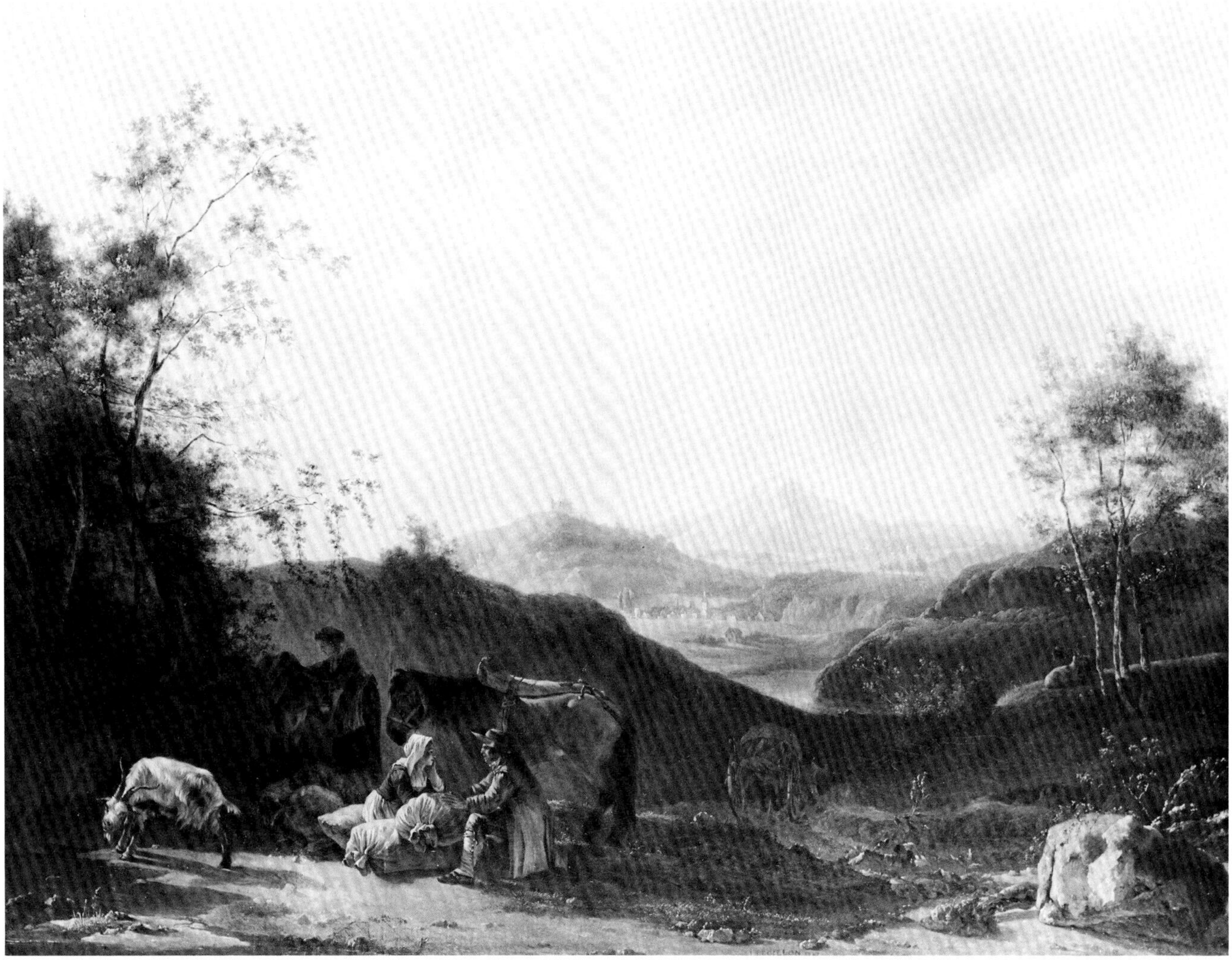

18

Fig. 7
Jean-Baptiste Legillon (1739–97)
*Landscape with Travelers*, 1787
Oil on canvas, 20½ x 27″
Gift of Calvin K. Arter, '36
1960.108

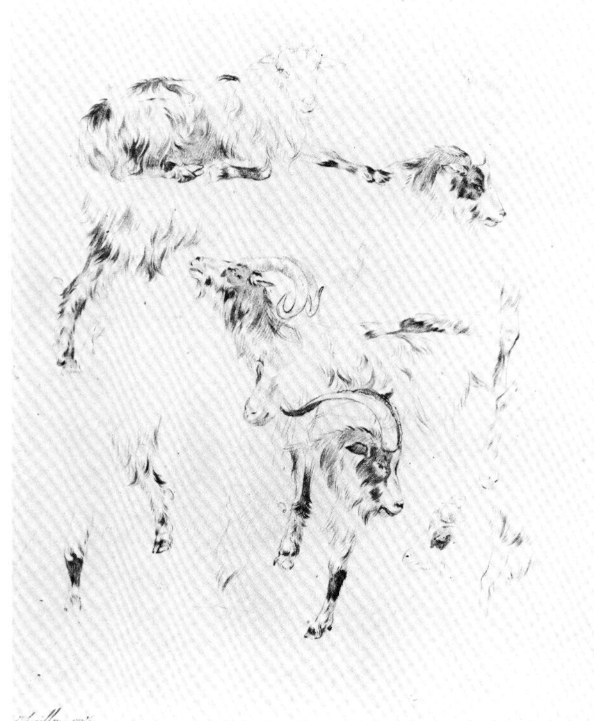

Fig. 8
Jean-Baptiste Legillon (1739–97)
*Studies of Goats*, 1786
Boymans-van Beuningen Museum, Rotterdam

1. André Félibien, *Entretiens sur les vies. . .* (Paris, 1685–88).

2. Oil on canvas, 35¾ x 28¾ in. (90.8 x 73 cm.).
Provenance: Neville Orgel Ltd, London; purchased 1978.
Exhibited: *The Rococo Age*, High Museum of Art, Atlanta, 1983, no. 17.
Bibliography: Alan P. Wintermutte, "Inventory of Paintings," *The First Painters of the King* (New York: Stair Sainty Matthiesen, 1985), p. 142, no. 147.

3. See Colombe Samoyault-Verlet, "Précisions iconographiques sur la salle du conseil de Fontainebleau," *La Revue du Louvre* (1974), p. 291, fig. 8.

4. The painter did exhibit an *Atelier of a Sculptor* in the Salon of 1747, and this is probably the work engraved by Marie-Madeleine Igonet in 1752, an impression of which is in the Print Department of the Metropolitan Museum of Art, New York. Another painting of the *Atelier of the Sculptor*, signed and dated by Pierre in 1756, was sold at the Hôtel Drouot in Paris, 26 March 1953, no. 111.

5. See the *Iconologie française* (1766; reprint 1976), p. 120.

6. See Fernand Engerand, *Inventaire des tableaux commandés et achetés par la direction des bâtiments du roi (1709–91)* (Paris, 1900), p. 450.

7. See Marc Sandoz, "Hughes Taraval," *Bulletin de la Société des beaux-arts de l'histoire et de l'art français 92* (1972), p. 230, no. 92. Among contemporary reviews, *La Prestesse, ou Nouvelle manière de prédire* (Paris, 1778), p. 15, called the painting "a bad parody of Boucher," but M. de Bachaumont, *Lettres sur les peintres* (London, 1780), p. 247, praised its freedom.

8. See Emil Dacier, *Catalogues des ventes et livrets des Salons illustrés par Gabriel de Saint-Aubin*, vol. IV (Paris, 1910), p. 47.

9. See Sandoz, p. 230, and also Peter Walch, "French Eighteenth-Century Oil Sketches from an English Collection," exhibition catalog, in *New Mexico Studies in the Fine Arts 60* (1980), p. 35. A work presumed to be a preliminary oil sketch was sold at the Galerie Georges Petit, Paris, 22 May 1922, no. 27; what appears to be a later replica is at the Tchevtchenko Gallery in Kazakhstan, Russia.

10. Oil on canvas, 50¾ x 38¼ in. (129 x 97 cm.).
Provenance: Taraval estate sale, Paris, 20 March 1786, no. 1; Arsène Houssaye; Sale Hôtel Drouot, Paris, 22–23 May 1896, no. 99; Sale Paris, 14–15 June 1920; L.-A. Gaboriand; Sale Hôtel Drouot, Paris, 25 June 1929, no. 54; Heim Gallery, London, by 1975; purchased 1976.
Exhibitions: Salon of 1781, Paris, no. 50; *The Rococo Age*, High Museum of Art, Atlanta, 1983, no. 21. Bibliography: Grete A. Kerlund, "Diderot och Hughes Taraval," *Ord or Bild* (1943); J. Seznec and J. Adhémar, *Diderot Salons*, vol. IV (Oxford, 1967), pp. 317–18; Sandoz, 1972, pp. 235–36, no. 112; Else Marie Bukdahl, *Diderot critique d'art* (Copenhagen, 1980), pp. 97 and 266, ill. 28; Joseph Baillio, "French Rococo Painting," *Apollo* (January 1984), p. 17.

11. As quoted in Seznec and Adhémar, p. 360: "Quand vous aurez dit de tous ces tableaux qu'il y a un peu de composition ajoutez que le reste est du dernier mauvais, et passez."

12. *La Peinturomanie, ou Cassandre au Salon, Comédie-parade en Vaudevilles* (Paris and Rome, 1781), p. 19; *Réflexions joyeuses d'un garçon de bonne humeur sur les tableaux exposés au Salon en 1781* (Paris, 1781), p. 15; *Galimatias anti-critique des tableaux de Salon* (The Hague, 1781), p. 17.

13. Carmotelle, *La Patte de velours* (London, 1781), pp. 29–30.

14. See *The First Painters of the King* (New York: Stair Sainty Matthiesen, 1985), no. 18.

15. Louis Petit de Bachaumont et al., "Première lettre," *Mémoires secrets* (1783), pp. 4–5; translated in Joseph Baillio, *Elizabeth Louise Vigée Le Brun* (Fort Worth, 1982), p. 8.

16. See Pierre Rosenberg *et al., French Painting 1774–1830: The Age of Revolution* (Paris, New York, and Detroit, 1974–75), no. 198.

17. See Stefano Susinno, "I ritratti degli accademici," in *L'Accademia Nazionale di San Luca* (Rome, 1974), p. 269, fig. 49; H. Bouchot, "Une artiste française pendant l'émigration," *Revue de l'art ancien et moderne* (1898), I, pp. 55–56; Pierre de Nolhac, *Madame Vigée-Le Brun* (Paris, 1908), II, between pp. 136–137.

18. Oil on canvas, 23¼ x 16⅝ in. (59 x 42 cm.).
Provenance: Gift of Charles K. Arter, Cleveland, 1961.
Exhibitions: *The Amherst Sesquicentennial Exhibition*, Hirschl and Adler Galleries, New York, 1972, no. 51; *Paintings from the Amherst College Collection*, Federal Reserve Board, Washington, D.C., 1981. According to Joseph Baillio in verbal communication, the later inscription "Virginia Le Brun" on the Accademia's painting resulted from a misunderstanding of her name, but was faithfully included in the copies, such as this one.

19. Oil on canvas, 18½ x 22 in. (49.9 x 55.8 cm.).
Provenance: Neville Orgel Ltd., London; purchased 1978.
Exhibition: *The Rococo Age*, High Museum of Art, Atlanta, 1983, no. 58.
Bibliography: Baillio, *Apollo* (1984), p. 21.

20. A. J. Dézallier d'Argenville, *Abrégé de la vie des plus fameux peintres*, vol. IV (Paris, 1762), p. 336.

21. *L'Atelier de Desportes* (Paris: Musée du Louvre, 1982–83).

22. See, for example, those reproduced in M. Faré, *La Nature morte en France* (Paris, 1962), II, pl. 312 (signed and dated 1736) and 313, and a pair of paintings also featuring dead birds at Heim, Paris, in June 1975. A nearly identical work, signed and dated 1739, was sold at the Palais Galliera, Paris, 28 March 1968; it differs only in the addition of some flowers to the basket of figs and in the absence of the carved relief.

23. See Jean Cailleux, "Themes and Survivals in Connection with Two Still Life Paintings by François Desportes," *The Burlington Magazine*, supplement (November 1969).

24. As a source of information on Legillon, see Denis Coekelberghs, *Les Peintres belges à Rome de 1700 à 1830* (Brussels and Rome, 1976), pp. 400–401.

25. Salon of 1789, Paris, no. 139. See Philip Conisbee, *Painting in Eighteenth-Century France* (Ithaca, 1981), p. 170, fig. 146.

26. Oil on canvas, 20½ x 27 in. (52 x 68.6 cm.).
Provenance: Gift of Calvin K. Arter, Cleveland, 1960.
Exhibition: *Paintings from the Amherst College Collection*, Federal Reserve Board, Washington, D.C., 1981.

27. Boymans-van Beuningen Museum, Rotterdam, ref. no. 2. Photo in the Frick Art Library, New York, Gernsheim no. 32, 153.

28. Other paintings are in Bruges and Warsaw, and another was reproduced in *Art et curiosité* (November 1967), p. 309.

# Other French Masterworks and their Artists

FRANK TRAPP & JUDITH A. BARTER

## CIRCLE OF NICOLAS POUSSIN
(French, 17th century)

A fine representation of *Narcissus* by the so-called "Hovingham Master" is one of two paintings acquired in recent years with an eye to their relationship to Nicolas Poussin (1593/4–1665). Although he spent most of his professional life in Rome, Poussin is universally accepted as the quintessential exponent of the classical principles upheld in French art of the Baroque period. At the same time, this impressive treatment of a subject from ancient classical mythology also reveals affinities with the art of Poussin's great compatriot Claude Gellée, called Claude Lorraine (1600–1682). Like Poussin, Claude spent most of his adult life in Rome, where he created an oeuvre that from his day onward has been regarded as the ultimate embodiment of the classical ideals in landscape. Inasmuch as authentic masterpieces by either of these great artists have by now become almost beyond reach even for major collections, we are the more fortunate in being able to present expressions of their principles by contemporaneous artists of lesser reputation but nevertheless admirable in their own right.

The portrayal of Narcissus now in the Mead Art Museum repeats the same composition as a picture in the Gemäldegalerie, Dresden, once considered to reveal the hand of Poussin himself. That canvas was procured for the Elector of Saxony in 1725, through an agent named Raymond Le Plat. Attribution of that picture and a number of other comparable works to a close follower of Poussin rather than to the master himself was proposed some years ago by the late Anthony Blunt, a leading modern authority on Poussin's work. Noting that these works differ from absolutely certain paintings by Poussin but that they closely follow upon that artist's "earlier, romantic style," Blunt pieced together a body of works that he believed to be attributable to the same maker. Because of common traits that related them to two canvases in the Worsley Collection at Hovingham Hall, Yorkshire, Blunt coined the sobriquet, "the Hovingham master" to refer to an artist presumed to have lived but no longer identifiable by proper name.[1] Although Blunt later reconsidered some of his original classifications of certain of these works deriving from the immediate circle of Poussin, he continued to regard the Dresden *Narcissus* and the one at Mead as attributable to the Hovingham Master.[2]

Blunt's notion of the Hovingham Master, however, has been challenged by other scholars. In her catalog of Poussin's work, Doris Wild attributes the Dresden version of the *Narcissus* to Jacques Stella (1596–1657), hence relating it to Poussin's early work.[3] On the other hand, Christopher Wright has in turn rejected Wild's proposal of that authorship, choosing instead to regard the painting as by a "competent follower no earlier than the mid 1630s."[4] Whatever the rights of the matter may turn out to be in the course of further discussion, the *Narcissus* now in the Mead Art Museum and its better known counterpart in Dresden reiterate the studied formalities of Poussin's learned pictorial commentaries on classical themes. Here, the subject, drawn from Ovid's *Metamorphoses*, concentrates upon what would prove the fatal self-involvement of the demigod as he stares at his own image in the waters. While the comparative directness of the iconography may in itself be indicative of another artist (Poussin delighted in intricacies of hidden meaning), some of the symbolism of the scene is still open to question. Who are the two female observers who watch with curious impassivity? Are they the nymphs of the stream Narcissus gazes into? Is it Echo, whose futile attentions were frustrated by Narcissus, who lurks nearby? Is she imprisoned in the rock or floating before it? In the distance is to be seen the figure of a faun, traditionally linked with fertility in classical lore. Still, his presence here, and that of the dog, remain puzzling.

All iconographical uncertainties aside, the scene presents a lyrical vision of a vanished antiquity steeped in the mysteries of life's passage. And for all its evocation of a sober, Poussinesque world, it is far from a purely derivative afterimage of that great master. A certain attenuated, mannered quality in the drawing—in the hands, for example, or in the elegantly cut silhouette of the hound—bespeaks the design of an artist of pronounced individualism. Poussin's forms are characteristically grander in scale, and, in recalling the soft, atmospheric qualities cultivated by Claude, the landscape setting itself also differs from Poussin's approach to nature. Stylistic fusions of the sort may well indicate the authorship of a sensitive admirer of both masters, working within the generally classical framework of the French Baroque. And whoever the painter of our Narcissus may have been, he came so close in spirit to the traditions nurtured by both Poussin and Claude that his very capable extension of their precepts makes his picture a most important asset for the Mead Art Museum.

F.T.

## REFERENCES

1. See Anthony Blunt, "Poussin Studies XII: The Hovingham Master," *The Burlington Magazine*, CIII, no. 704 (November 1961): 454–461.

2. Mead Art Museum Document File, report from the Heim Gallery, London, 1977.

3. Doris Wild, *Nicolas Poussin, Katalog der Werke* (Zurich: Orell Füssli Verlag, 1980), vol. II, p. 282.

4. Christopher Wright, *Poussin Paintings, A Catalogue Raisonné* (New York: Hippocrene Books, 1985), p. 241.

*Editor's Note:*

In correspondence on the subject of this painting and its attribution, Eric Zafran has made a number of helpful suggestions about bibliography and interpretation, for which warm thanks are due.

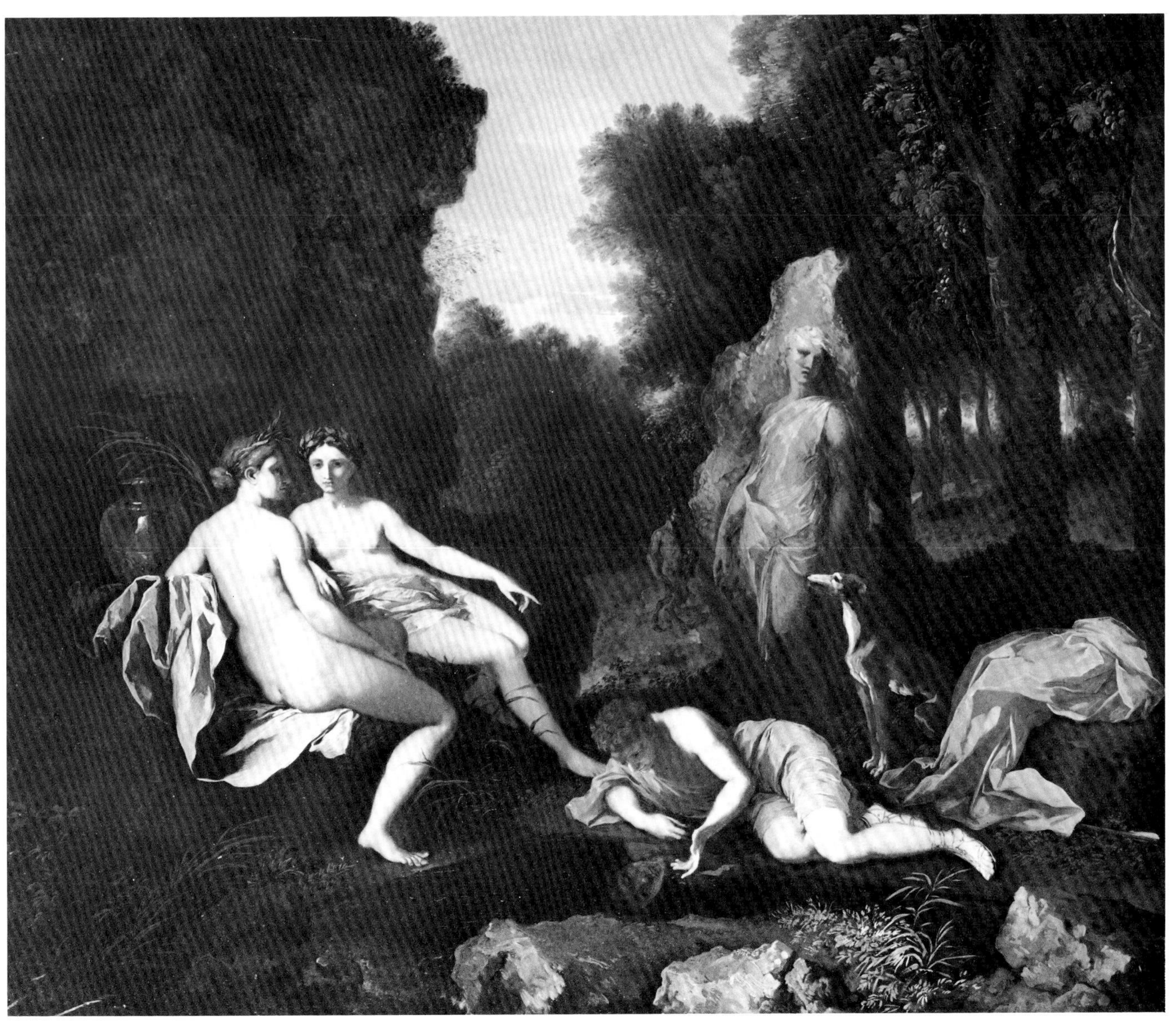

*Narcissus {and Echo and Two Nymphs}*
Oil on canvas, 30 x 34″
Museum purchase
1977.2

## REYNAUD LEVIEUX (1620–90)

This *Holy Family* by Reynaud Levieux is in many respects closer to the exacting mold of Nicolas Poussin's art than is the Mead's circle-of-Poussin *Narcissus.* Substantially present in it is something closely akin to Poussin's serene and sober approach to devotional themes, though personal nuances of style and expression that experts recognize as special to Levieux are also detectable. As in works by Poussin himself, strong overtones of Raphael's art abound here—the more so, perhaps, in Levieux's rather tender characterization of the sacred personages present, and in their muted air of involvement with each other. With all their attention centered on the Christ Child in their midst, they exude the qualities of sweet but restrained sentiment traditionally admired in Raphael's art, which Poussin, too, so admired and wished to emulate. Although less monumental in impact than their counterparts in comparable compositions by Poussin, Levieux's figures share more of the sculptural convictions to be expected in a Poussin than do the slighter and more mannered beings in the *Narcissus.* And the landscape also bears a closer resemblance to Poussin's own interpretations of classical landscape, whatever his sources of inspiration in actual models may have been. Resemblances to such antique masterpieces as the "Odyssey Landscapes," now in the Vatican Museum Library, are more tantalizing to observe than specifically edifying, for those striking specimens of authentic Roman landscape painting were not unearthed until 1840 and 1849. But in the meantime, much also has presumably been lost, so the question of what the ancient models for Renaissance and Baroque art may in fact have been remains to some extent conjecture.

A native of the Provençal city of Nîmes, where his father was established as a goldsmith, Levieux studied the painter's craft in Rome, where he remained from 1640 to 1644. He was especially impressed by the paintings of Raphael and Poussin that he encountered there. Although he initiated an independent career in Nîmes following his sojourn in Rome, he returned to the papal city in 1655, and again from 1668 to 1671, so he kept abreast of artistic developments in that cosmopolitan center. The bulk of his surviving production remains in the vicinity of Nîmes, Aix-en-Provence, and Avignon,

*The Holy Family*
 *(with Saint John the Baptist)*
Oil on canvas
31¾ x 29¾″
Museum purchase
1980.30

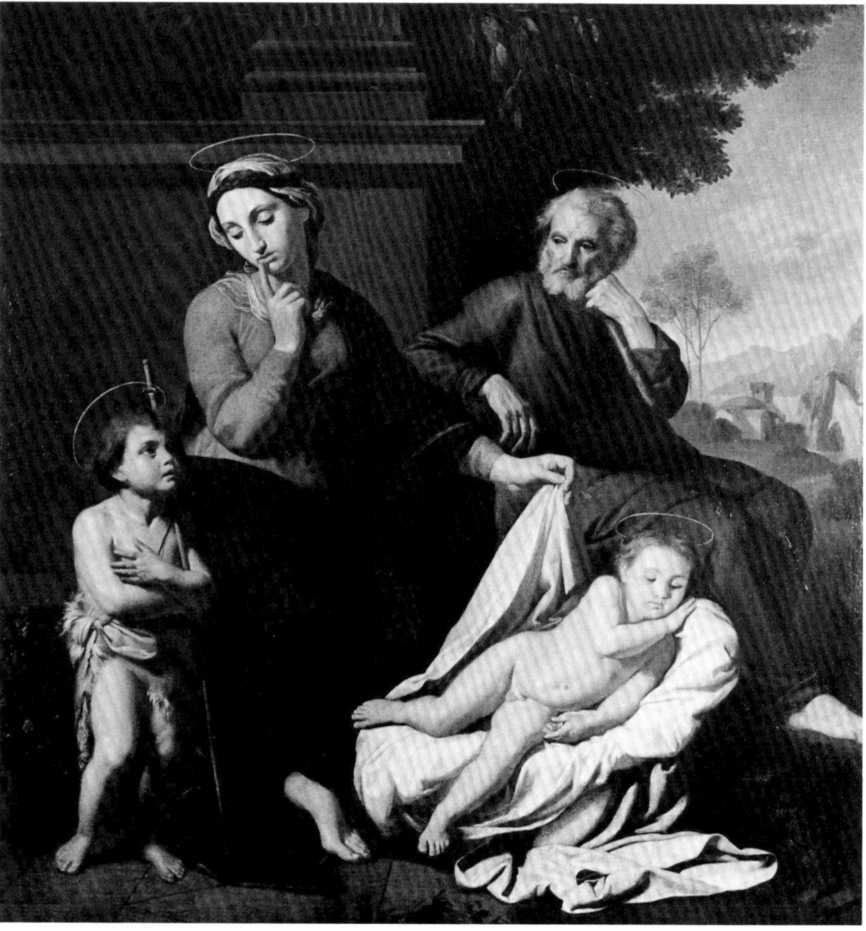

where he was employed over the years. Strong similarities of style and resemblances of facial type would seem to link the Mead *Holy Family* with other paintings still to be seen in collections in the artist's home country. Sometimes considered the masterpiece of this important Provençal master, this particular composition may well date from the years 1650–1660, when the painter worked at Avignon. In the context of the Amherst College Collection it has the special interest of affording a pendant to the *Narcissus*, in which two sides of the tradition of Poussin may be admired in paintings by lesser but highly capable masters of the Baroque era in France.

F.T.

## HYACINTH RIGAUD (1659–1743)

There were, of course, sides of artistic production in France of the Baroque period that cannot yet be represented in the Amherst College Collection. It is to be hoped, for example, that in due course we shall be able to call upon the rich if chilly interpretations of religious, historical, and mythological subjects turned out by the small army of academic court artists maintained by the state. The same is to be said for exponents of less pretentious categories of subject matter such as landscape, genre, and still life. Those who supplied the demands of the rather different clientele for these less formal kinds of art include painters of such enduring reputation as the brothers Le Nain.

At least we are able to muster the presence of the sovereign figure of that age, King Louis XIV himself, in a portrayal by one of his favorite portraitists, Hyacinth Rigaud. Born in Perpignan and first trained as an artist in the provinces, Rigaud made his way to Paris and enrolled in the academy in 1782. Although he harbored ambitions to become a history painter, his talents as a portraitist were recognized by Charles Le Brun (1619–90), who wielded great influence in court circles. Rigaud was thus diverted from his original desire to pursue further studies in Rome. His success in the art of portraiture was virtually all-consuming from then on, and his name has been forever associated with representations of the Sun King and other notable

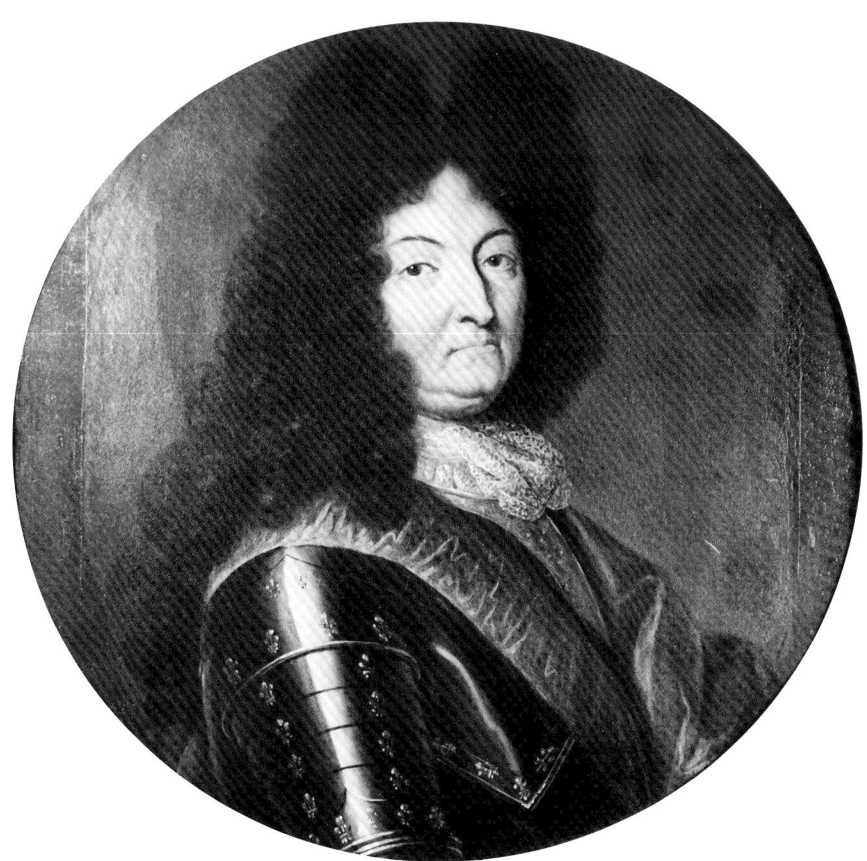

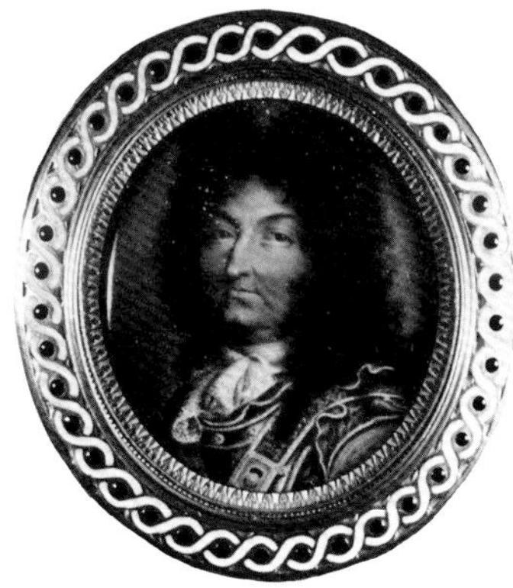

**JEAN PETITOT** (1607/8–91)
*Portrait of Louis XIV (1638–1715)*
Enamel on gold, miniature
1¾ x 1½″ with inner frame, as illustrated
Gift of Miss Susan Dwight Bliss
1958.116


*Portrait of Louis XIV*, c. 1690
Oil on canvas
28″ in diameter
Gift of Charles H. Morgan
1941.20

figures of his time. Thanks to wide distribution of reproductive engravings after his most famous subjects, his reputation was international in scope, and many of the formulas he invented were perpetuated as far away as the American republic yet to come. (Gilbert Stuart's ''Lansdowne'' portrait of Washington, 1796, faithfully repeats the essential structure of a composition by Rigaud.)

Although painted just before the turn of the eighteenth century, Rigaud's image of Louis XIV conserves the air of vigor and pride persistently fostered during that monarch's long years of reign. The king's alert and commanding mien was tirelessly counterfeited by capable portraitists like Rigaud in official portraits for distribution throughout France and abroad. The portrait now at the Mead is exemplary of the high level of craft maintained in this virtually ceaseless production. In some ways more engaging to modern eyes, however, perhaps by virtue of its precious size and material, is another image of the king executed in miniature by Jean Petitot (1607/8–91), which is also in the Amherst College Collection. In both cases, the features of that domineering figure on the world stage of the time assume a lively sense of presence that helps span the many years that divide his age from our own.

F.T.

It is only in recent years that the accomplishments of French artists of the late eighteenth and early nineteenth centuries have received the serious study they deserve. One of the beneficiaries of that renewal of critical attention is Nicolas-Antoine Taunay (1755–1830), the author of *The Finding of Moses* recently purchased for the Mead Art Museum. A protégé though not an actual pupil of the famous Rococo master Jean-Honoré Fragonard (1732–1806), Taunay initiated a successful career, culminating in his appointment to the Institut de France at the time of its founding, in 1795. He enjoyed particular favor during the Empire, when he was one of the Empress Josephine's cultural circle. After Napoleon's fall from power, Taunay accepted an invitation, in 1816, to help establish an academy of fine arts in Rio de Janeiro. He remained there for five years. Eventually disillusioned by that experience, he returned to Paris in 1821, regaining his seat at the Institute and the honors befitting that station.

Dating from the artist's years in Brazil, *The Finding of Moses* is one of many compositions in which his direct studies of the flora of that land lend an exotic charm to his biblical interpretations. In this case, his invention of a ''fluvial landscape''[1] as a setting for his Old Testament narrative is especially appropriate. An earlier version of a painting of the same subject now in the

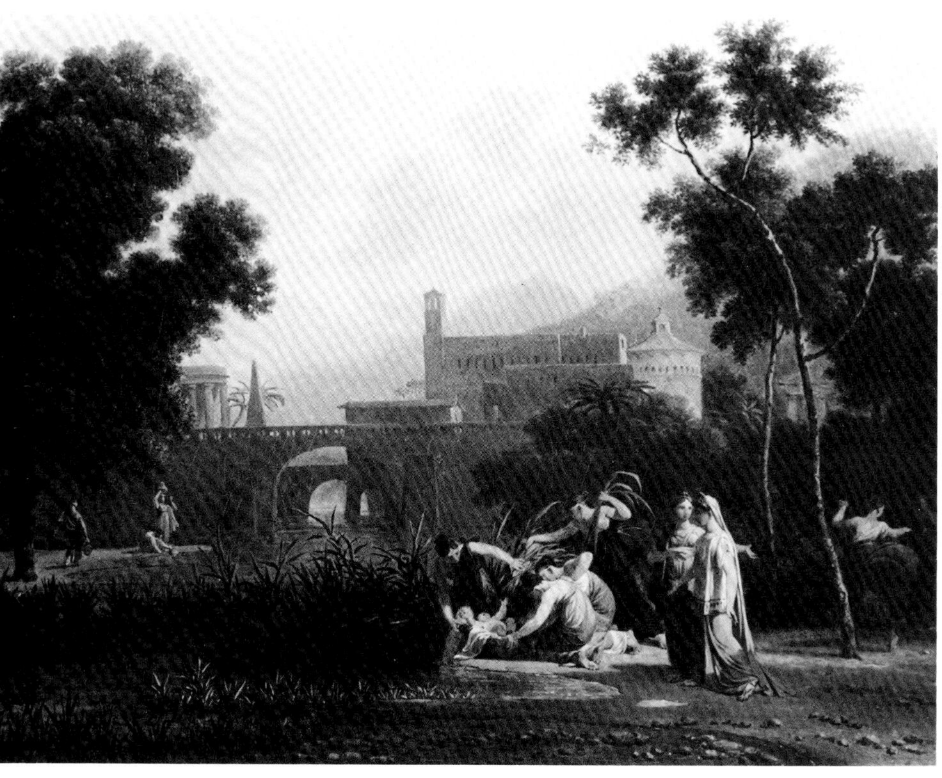

*The Finding of Moses;*
Salon of 1827
Oil on canvas
12¼ x 15½ "
Museum purchase
1987.3

## LOUIS HERSENT (1777–1860)

Museu Nacional de Belas Artes, Rio de Janeiro, the picture now at Mead was shown at the Salon of 1827 in Paris (no. 979, *Moïse sauvé des eaux*), and was part of the posthumous sale of the contents of the artist's studio, in 1831.[2] In more recent times the Mead picture was mistaken—quite understandably—for a work by the distinguished Neoclassical landscapist Jean-Victor Bertin (1775–1842), but its true authorship has since been reliably established. In it, the qualities of luminous, expansive vistas cultivated in the classical tradition of landscape painting happily fuse with engaging narrative and topographical touches that bear the stamp of the artist's unusual personal experiences.

F.T.

1. For a discussion of Taunay, see exhibition catalog, *French Painting 1774–1830: The Age of Revolution*, Detroit Institute of Arts, 5 March–4 May 1975; Metropolitan Museum of Art, New York, 12 June–7 September 1975. The discussion of *The Sermon of Saint John the Baptist* especially relates to the subject at hand.

2. See Hazlitt, Gooden, and Fox, *French Paintings from 1800 to 1850*, exhibition catalog, 16 March–19 April 1984, pp. 6–7. The catalog cites the following discussions of the attribution of the picture: Suzanne Gutwirth, "Jean-Victor Bertin, un paysagiste neo-classique," *Gazette des beaux-arts* LXXIII (May–June 1974), p. 348, no. 70 (illustrated as Bertin); Suzanne Gutwirth, "A Pre-Romantic Painting by Nicolas-Antoine Taunay," *Bulletin of the Los Angeles County Museum of Art*, 1979, p. 36.

Much honored in his day, Louis Hersent pursued a productive career in which initial efforts conforming to the strict precepts of Jacques Louis David and the French academy were progressively extended to include modern and exotic themes alongside those of the classical past. Hersent enjoyed particular popularity after the fall of Napoleon, at the time of the restoration of the Bourbons, when, under the patronage of the royal family, he undertook themes full of flattering political overtones. One of his large canvases presented at the Salon of 1817 shows him in this guise of dynastic apologist. Representing *Louis XVI Distributing Alms to the Poor*, his subject was a thinly veiled effort to associate that unfortunate monarch with his younger brother and eventual successor, King Louis XVIII.

*Gustave Wasa (King of Sweden)* represents a less obvious but no less politically charged scene. King Gustave was the founder of an independent Swedish nation. It was he who ordered the Swedish translation of the Bible that first fixed the native Swedish tongue. Here he is shown at the end of his life, as he returns from exile at the court of Denmark. Analogies with the restoration of the House of Bourbon to the throne of France were readily drawn by the Salon public of Hersent's day. His canvas was honored with a gold medal at the Salon of 1819, and its reputation and that

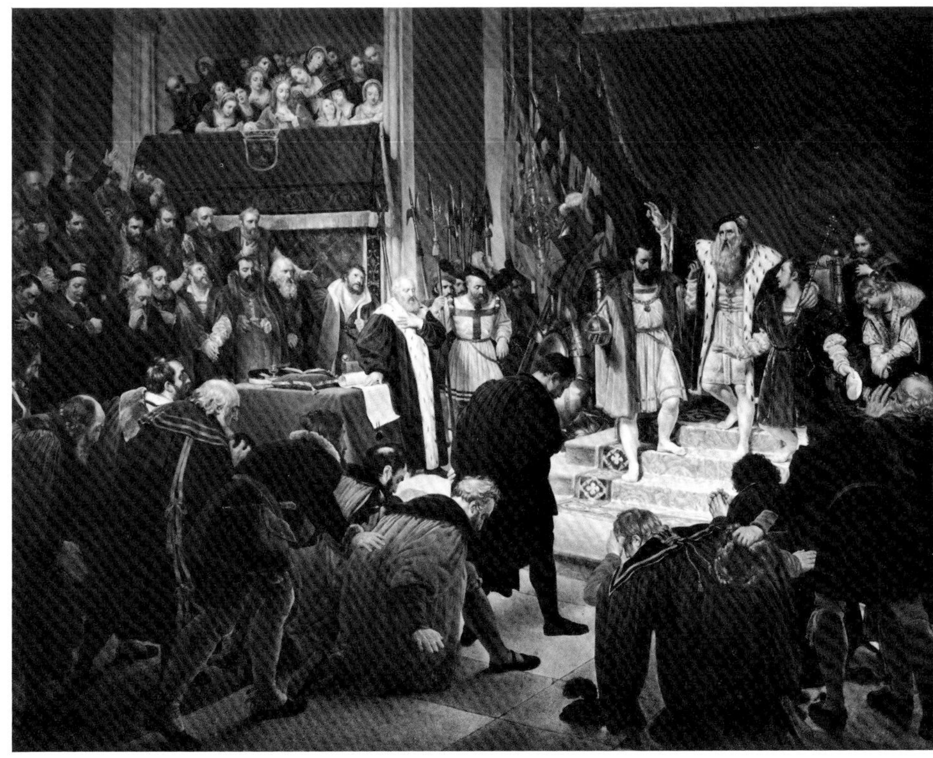

*Gustave Wasa* after 1819
Oil on canvas
34 11/16 x 42 1/2 "
Museum purchase
1984.23

of its maker were perpetuated by copies in print form. The subject matter aside, it is easy to understand how viewers attuned to the values promulgated in the later forms of French Neoclassicism would have been impressed with the ceremonial dignity of Hersent's composition, and with the artist's lavish attention to historical costume. It is also understandable that at the time of the Revolution of 1848 and the overthrow of the incumbent, Orleanist King Louis-Philippe, political leanings of the sort were popularly resented, so that Hersent's picture was destroyed when the Palais Royal was set afire by revolutionary iconoclasts. The smaller version of the same subject now in the collection of the Mead Art Museum is regarded as a faithful copy made as a studio record of the much-esteemed Salon piece. The high quality of its technical execution argues for the close involvement of the master himself in the production of the work.

F.T.

Louise Joséphine Sarazin de Belmont (1790–1870) enjoyed a long and successful career as a painter of landscapes and architectural subjects. One of the best pupils of Pierre-Henri Valenciennes (1750–1819), she was schooled in the traditions of heroic landscape maintained by that master. Her command of the principles of classical landscape painting is beautifully demonstrated in the picture now in the Mead. Signed, and dated 1820, it was exhibited as no. 1165 at the Paris Salon of 1822, where Delacroix's controversial *Dante and Virgil* also appeared. De Belmont's entry was more in harmony with the tastes of the day, however, despite the romantic nature of its literary source and its evidences of the so-called "troubadour" fashion popularized by Ingres and other individualistic exponents of Neoclassicism. Traits of the sort are to be detected in the balletic mannerisms of the figures and in the forecasts of gothicism in the castle toward which their way leads. Although they are now less famous than their great English counterpart J. M. W. Turner (1775–1851), de Belmont and her mentors served to sustain the afterimage of the Claudean landscape tradition, which would enjoy so vigorous a rebirth in Romantic landscape painting of the nineteenth century, not least of all in the hands of such exponents of historical landscape as Thomas Cole. Indeed, the rapports of conception and feeling between de Belmont's *Gil Blas and Don Alfonso* and Cole's *Time Past* and *Time Present*, also in our collection, are fascinating to contemplate.

The subject derives from that rambling, picaresque account, *The Adventures of Gil Blas of Santillane*, published in the eighteenth century by Alain René Lesage (1668–1747). Derived of Spanish models but peculiarly French in tone, the tales of Lesage's attractive rogue (like those of his counterpart, Figaro) enjoyed a widespread popularity throughout Europe, one that persisted well into the nineteenth century. De Belmont portrays a scene from book VI chapter 3, in which Gil Blas and Don Alphonso, his companion of the time, approach a fanciful castle, as they travel toward Valencia on their way to Italy. Quite by chance they encounter the Baron Steinback, Don Alphonso's adoptive father, who conducts them to the castle. There the baron introduces Don Alphonso to his true father, Don Caesar de Levya, the owner of the castle, which will be part

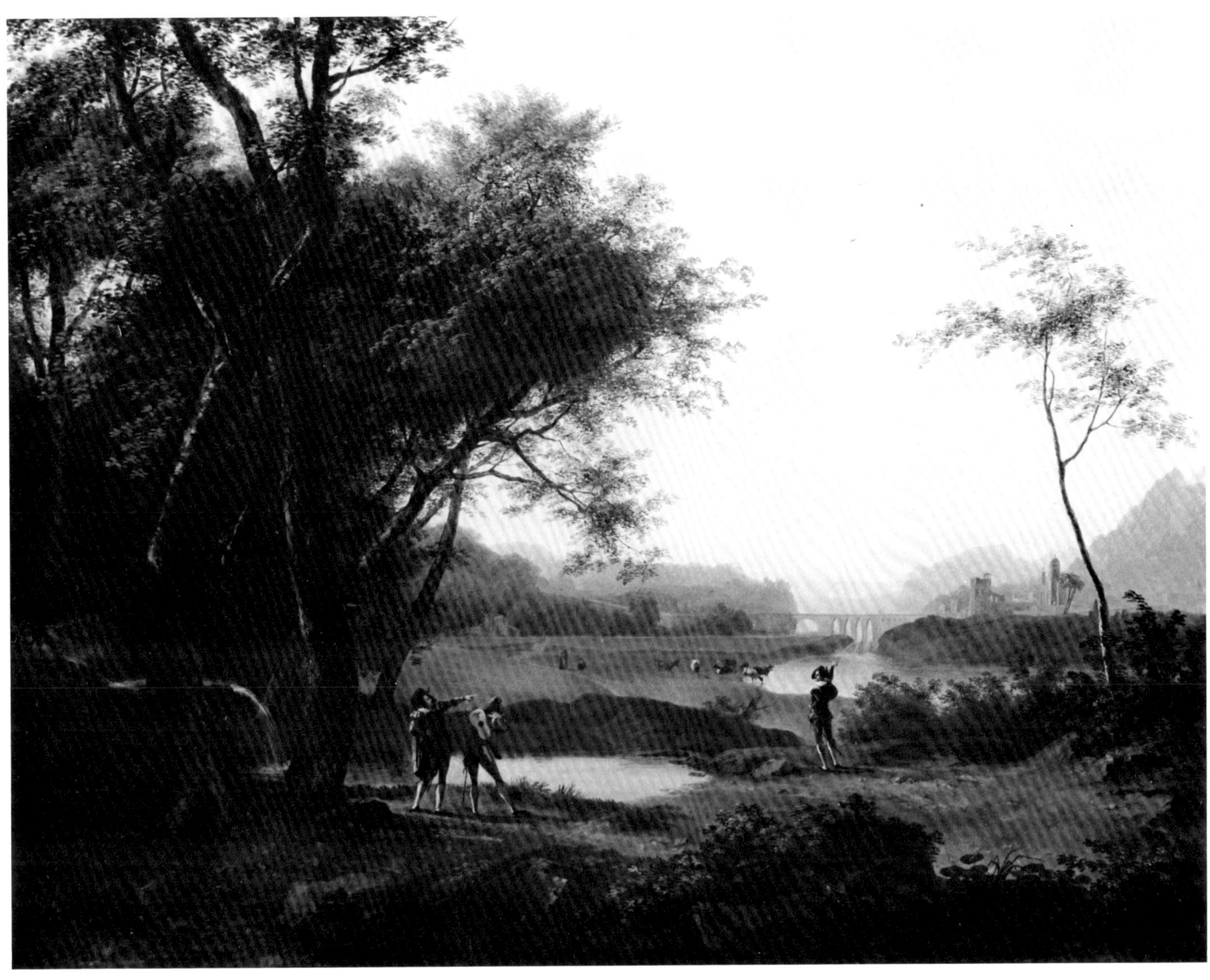

of Don Alphonso's proper birthright. After sharing this happy news with his friend, Gil Blas is prepared to resume his wanderings alone in search of yet another adventure.

Just how often de Belmont undertook subjects from *Gil Blas* cannot now be said. One other composition derived from the same literary source has in recent years turned up in the market and is now part of a private collection in Europe. Although the Mead Art Museum canvas dates from fairly early in the painter's career, it reveals mature powers of artistic command. Those creative powers were sustained throughout a long and productive career, during which de Belmont was regularly represented at the Paris Salon and was twice singled out for special honors.

F.T.

*Gil Blas and Don Alphonso Arriving at the Castle,* 1820
Oil on canvas
25 ½  x  31 ¾ "
Museum purchase
1987

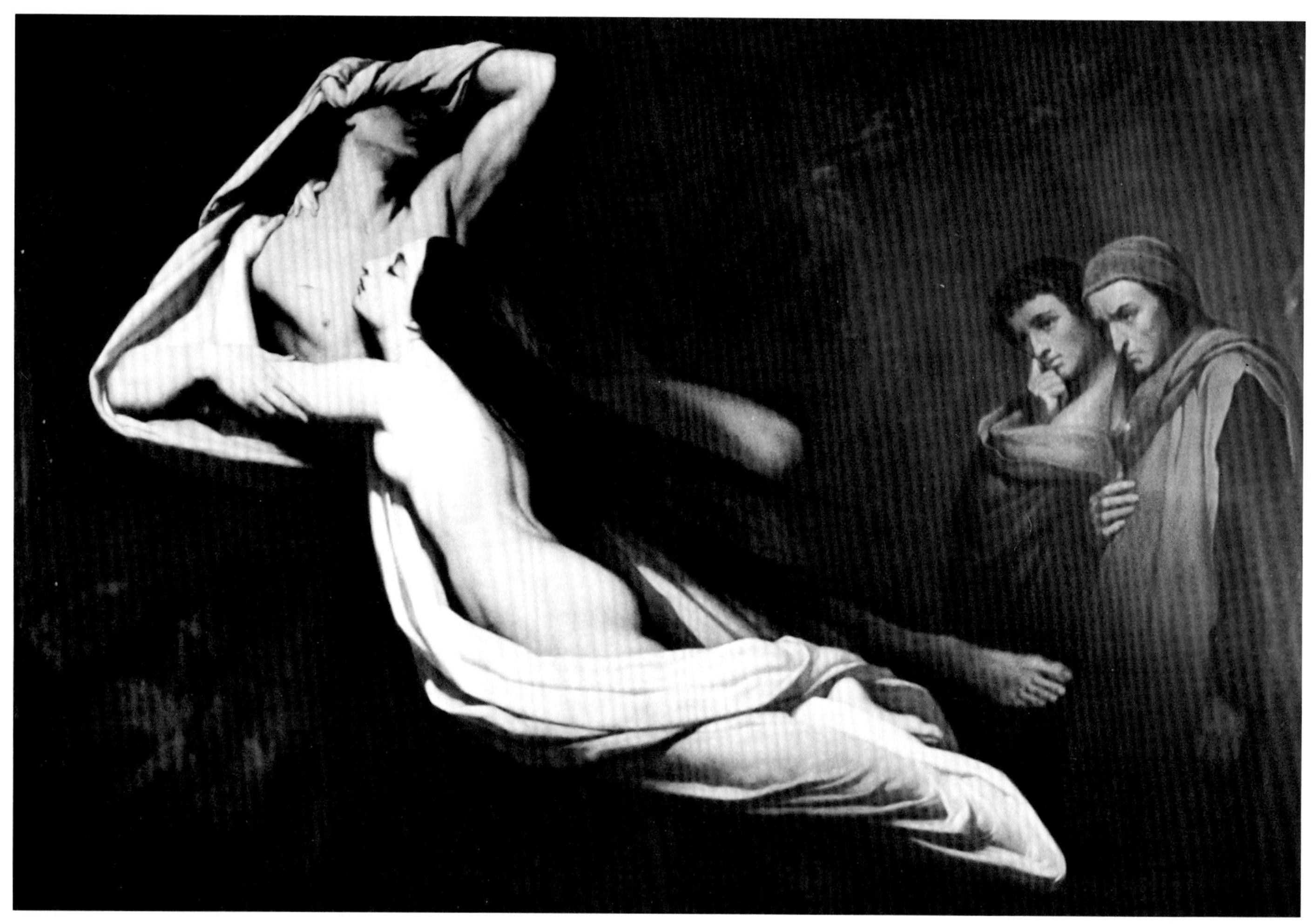

## ARY SCHEFFER (1795–1858)

Although born in Dordrecht, Holland, of mixed Ger-
man and Dutch parentage, Scheffer is now accounted
as one of the Romantic generation of French painters.
After initial training with his father, he enrolled briefly with Pierre-Paul Prud'hon (1758–1823), and then
in the studio of the well-known Neoclassical master
Pierre-Narcisse Guérin (1774–1833), whose pupils also
included Géricault and Delacroix. Like those more illustrious classmates, Scheffer ventured into a vein of
subjective interpretation that earned him the admira-
tion of those who had defected from the ideological
constraints of strictly academic practice. At times, as
in his moving *Death of Géricault*, 1825, now in the
Louvre, he indulged in the freer, more painterly sur-

faces associated with the Romantic school. In *Paolo and Francesca*, however, the lateral emphasis of the composition, the comparative polish of the surface, and the linear definition of the forms recall modes encouraged by the older generation, whose values Scheffer never wholly repudiated. His atmospheric treatment of the glowing fires of the infernal city and the ghostly presence of floating figures in the distance are, on the other hand, more in line with the painterly effects cultivated by Delacroix and the Romantics. Scheffer's mixed allegiances are particularly appreciable in the subject at hand, where the sentimental flair that earned him favor in the eyes of his royal patrons is fluently implemented.

Throughout his career, Scheffer exhibited intense devotion to poetic subject matter drawn from the pages of Dante, Byron, Goethe, Schiller, Scott, and other idols of the Romantic era. Those enthusiasms showed themselves early, as here, in a subject from Canto 5 of Dante's *Inferno.* The scene takes place in an ideal year of 1300. The love affair between Francesca da Rimini and her brother-in-law, Paolo Maletesta, has been discovered by Francesca's husband, Lanciotti Maletesta, an ill-favored hunchback, who has taken revenge by stabbing both lovers to death. Now in Hell, Dante and Virgil gaze upon the doomed lovers.

Perhaps inspired by the drawings of the British artist John Flaxman (1755–1826), whose illustrations of Dante were internationally popular at the time, Scheffer shows the famous scene of the doomed lovers. His original version of the subject was intended for inclusion in the Salon of 1822, where Delacroix's more controversial *Dante and Virgil* appeared, but was actually completed much later. Scheffer painted a number of replicas of this popular composition. The version now in the Mead Art Museum appears to have been painted, perhaps with the aid of assistants, at the time when exhibits for the Paris Universal Exposition of 1855 were being prepared. Aside from the original canvas in the Louvre, a slightly larger replica is now in the Wallace Collection, London, while preparatory versions are to be seen in the Ary Scheffer Museum, Dordrecht; in the Musée Borgoin, Clermont-Ferrand; and in the Cleveland Museum of Art.

## Editor's Note:

The document file of the Museum includes the following comments on this picture, submitted by the dealer at the time of the purchase: "Mrs. Grote, who compiled the Life of Ary Scheffer in 1860, writes about the Wallace Collection painting and of this 1854 replica. She relates seeing the earlier one in Ary Scheffer's studio about twenty years after he had painted it, when it was there for restoration. This was circa 1852–55, and while Ary Scheffer was actually painting this 1854 canvas. Her words are quoted, in part: "In the spring of the year 1854. . .I was a visitor at the residence of Scheffer. . .and there beheld the second 'replica' which may be regarded, in truth, as *surpassing in point of execution the first Francesca*. . .while the delicate, minute details of drapery, texture, etc., were also executed by the master himself. . . ."

F.T.

*Paolo and Francesca*, 1854
Oil on canvas
45 x 64"
Museum purchase
1965.110

**ANDRÉ GIROUX** (1801–79)

Trained at the École des Beaux-Arts, Paris, André Giroux made his professional debut at the Salon of 1819, where he showed genre subjects. But it was as a landscape painter that he won his spurs as an artist: in 1825 he was awarded the Salon's first grand prize for historical landscape. The small painting now in the Mead Art Museum dates from that early stage of his life, when he embarked on travels that took him to Rome, Naples, and other parts of Italy. Those destinations were natural for an aspiring young artist of that era, when the traditions of classical landscape painting were fervently nurtured at the Académie Française in Rome. A portrait of Giroux, painted by an unidentified hand during the period of Giroux's residence there, remains at this academy to recall his student days in Italy. The qualities his work displays of classical clarity and constraint of composition and color, qualities fostered by the contemporary doyens of landscape painting in the classical tradition,[1] were no less enthusiastically adopted by the young Camille Corot (1796–1875) during his own first visit to Italy, in the years 1825–27. Indeed, Giroux's small landscape closely resembles Corot's efforts of the time, both in quality and in kind.

Within its small format, Giroux's scene admirably captures the sweep of the famous Bay of Naples as it was to be seen from the heights of Cape Misene. Like his ultimately more famous compatriot Corot, Giroux continued to utilize subject matter drawn from his extensive travels, whether in Italy or in parts of France and Switzerland. His landscapes continued to earn him favorable attention throughout a long and active career as an exhibitor at the Paris Salon, where he continued to be represented until the 1860s.

F.T.

1. Here the names of Pierre-Henri Valenciennes, Jean-Victor Bertin, and Caruelle d'Aligny (1798–1871) come to mind as representative of that flourishing school. A drawing of Nemi by D'Aligny, recently acquired for the College collection, exemplifies the qualities to be appreciated in the drawings that Corot and other artists of the Neoclassical persuasion made on visits to those parts of the picturesque Italian countryside.

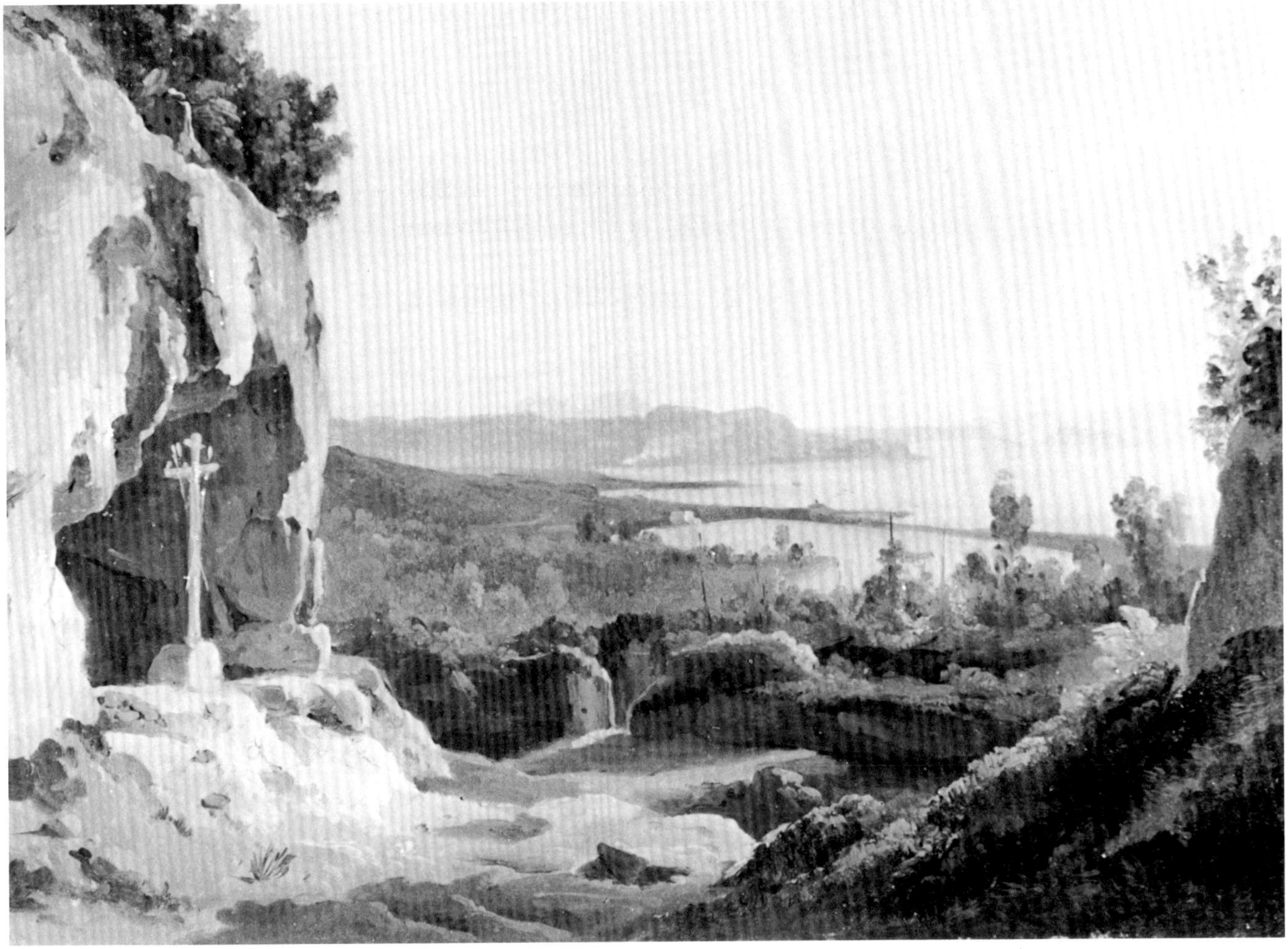

*A View of the Bay of Naples From Cape Misene*, c. 1825
Oil on paper laid on canvas
11¾  x 8¾ "
Museum purchase
1984.16

Claude Felix Théodore d'Aligny (1798–1871)
      (called Caruelle d'Aligny)
*Nemi*
Pencil
10 x 13⅝"
Museum purchase
1987.5

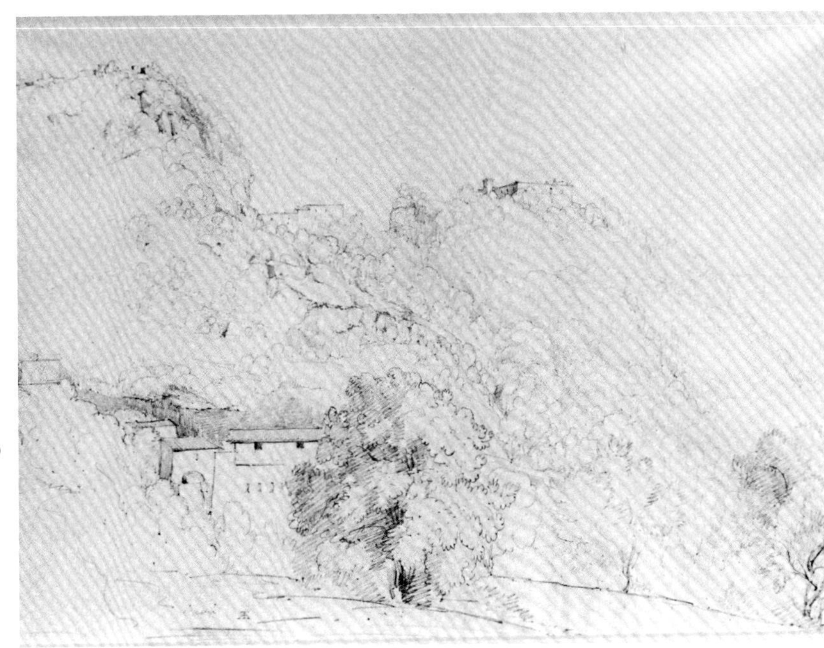

## LOUIS GABRIEL EUGÈNE ISABEY (1803–86)

Another member of the so-called Romantic generation, Eugène Isabey was first schooled in art by his father, Jean-Baptiste Isabey (1767–1855), who was well-known as a portrait miniaturist and lithographer.[1] The son initiated his own career as an artist at the Salon of 1824, where he showed landscape and marine compositions, a range of subject that would continue to provide his main source of inspiration. Engaged in 1830 as a draftsman to accompany a government deputation to Algeria, he anticipated by two years the direct experience of Islam that so indelibly affected the art of his colleague Delacroix. Indeed, when the latter visited North Africa in his turn, it was because Isabey had declined an invitation to accompany a second French mission charged to restore diplomatic ties with the hostile sultan of Morocco. For Isabey, northerly climes retained the hold they had gained during his youthful associations with such British friends as the gifted Richard Parkes Bonington (1802–28). For years to come, Isabey continued to be drawn to coastal subjects, which he often gave a dramatic, stormy air. His *Beach at Honfleur*, 1827, or *The Port of Dunkerque*, 1831, typify those interests, which would persist in the repertory of later French artists.

In later years, however, history painting also came to attract Isabey, as is attested in his well-known depiction, *King Louis-Philippe of France Receiving Queen Victoria at Tréport*, 1846, or his picturesque reenactment, *The Marriage of Henry IV*, painted two years afterward. A late historical fantasy, *The Temptation of Saint Anthony*, 1869, is more in character with the subject matter treated in the painting now at the Mead Art Museum. Known at the time of its purchase simply as a scene of the Inquisition, this latter canvas may in fact prove to have more specific literary associations. Given the popularity of the Faust legend in the Romantic epoch—it was often interpreted by artists, writers, and musicians—one might reasonably suspect that Isabey's dramatic scene is actually that of Margarite's trial, with the infant's crib shown in an accusingly prominent placement on the stage. Whatever the case, this agitated scene, with its effective painterly handling, serves as a reminder of the theatrical side of high Romanticism in French art of the nineteenth century.

F.T.

1. Jean-Baptiste Isabey's accomplishments as a lithographer are represented in the print collection at Mead.

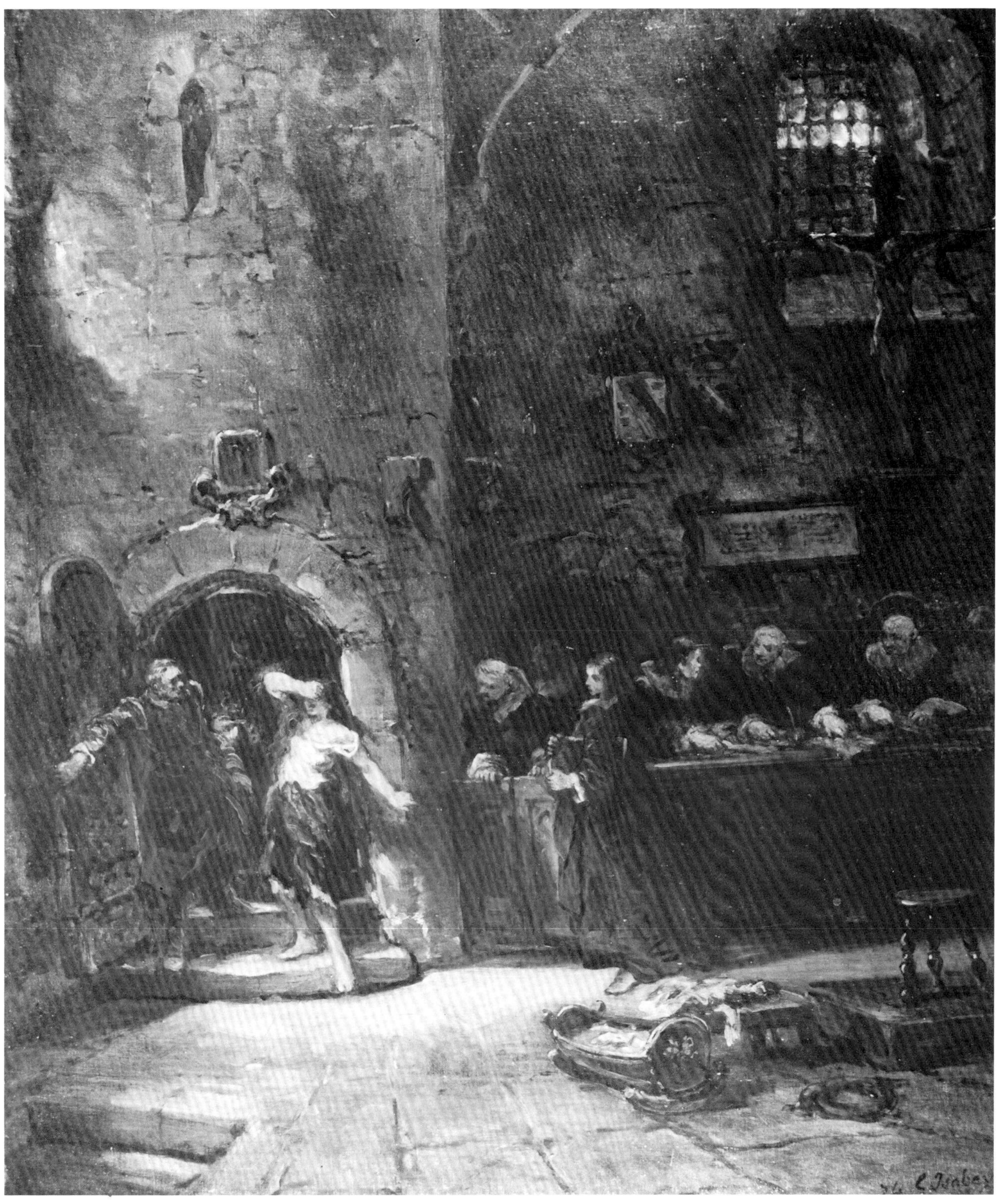

*Inquisition Scene*, 1874
Oil on canvas
23 ¾ x 29″
Museum purchase
1977.55

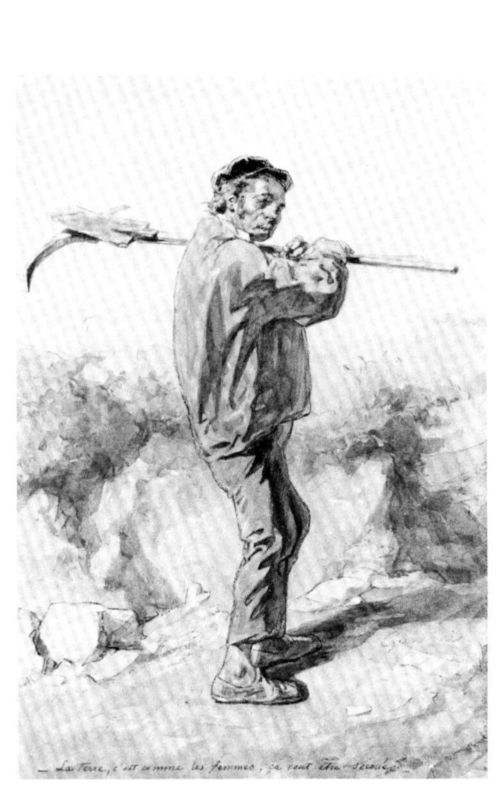

*A Worker*
Watercolor, 8¼ x 12¼ ″
Museum purchase
1971.32

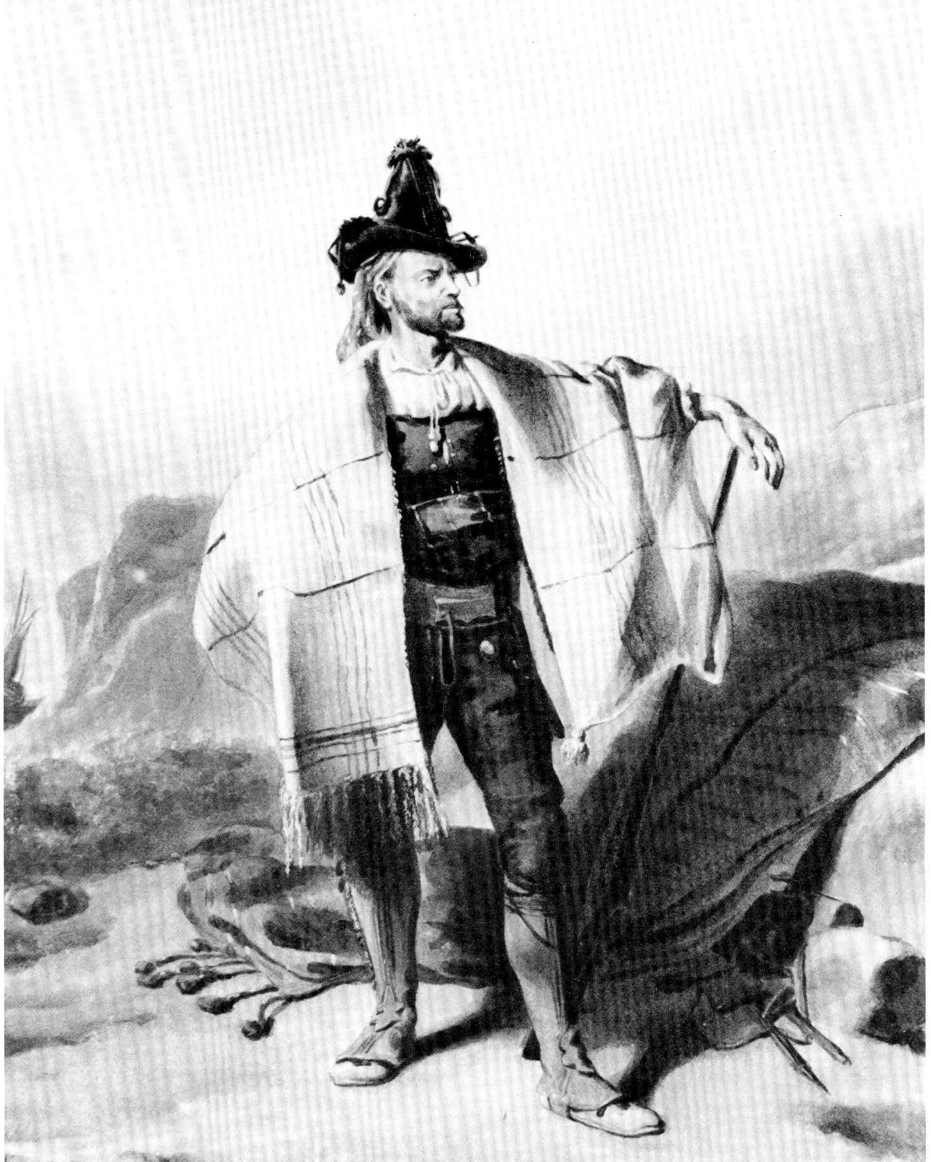

*Le Contrebandier,* 1836
Gouache and watercolor, 21½ x 16¾ ″
Museum purchase
1986.37

# PAUL GAVARNI (1804–66)

Born Sulpice Guillaume Chevalier in Paris, "Gavarni" took his *nom de guerre* from a picturesque landscape watercolor of the Pyrenees entitled *Gavarnie*, which he submitted to the 1829 Salon. Through an error, the name of the place was given as the name of the artist, and he used it ever after. In fact, the use of the new name signaled a turning point in his career. In 1829 Gavarni took a studio in Montmartre and began producing sketches of picturesque landscapes and costumes. The revolution of 1830 gave impetus to the growth of Romanticism, and the newly enfranchised populace showed an interest in picturesque "types" and costumes associated with the common man, as well as in nostalgic fantasies of other periods and places. Gavarni's expertise at costume design earned him a place on the staff of Emile de Girardin's *La Mode.* He also designed for dressmakers and the theater, and contributed to *L'Artiste.* In 1833 he attempted to start his own publication, *Le Journal des gens du monde*, but after its failure he spent two years in debtors' prison.

Around 1836–37 Gavarni began to draw humorous satirical sketches of social customs and manners for *Charivari*, works that have often been compared to those of Daumier. He was a sharp social critic, and compared the lives of rich and poor with a socialistic sensibility. This viewpoint led him to a more and more trenchant political satire directed at bourgeois values. His work was admired by Gautier and collected by Degas.

Nineteenth-century depictions of peasants or exotic types often reflect their makers' committed interest in a different way of life, and the artists' respect for those who lived marginally at the edge of capitalism and commercialization. Indeed, artists such as Gavarni, Daumier, Millet, and Jongkind created an empathic bridge between their subjects and the middle-class urban buyers of their pictures. For the early and mid-19th-century Romantic painters, peasant, worker, or ethnic subjects reflected a system of breadwinning by individual hard labor that they believed superior to the usury of urban capitalism.

Gavarni's *contrebandier*, or smuggler, is an exotic, proud, commanding type who lives outside the bourgeois legal system. In fact, he earns his living by cheating that system, by subverting its capitalist drive. As an individual, he defies a society that excludes him, and he chooses risk and opportunity as a way of life. His cigarette tossed on the ground and still burning, the ship waiting in the background, and his strewn-about goods all point to his immediate and transient life-style.

Amherst is fortunate to own another watercolor by the same artist. *The Worker* is typical of Gavarni's later work of the 1850s; this rendering of a laborer carrying his pickax and shovel also recalls Millet's peasants of the late 1860s. Gavarni's figure lacks the more statuesque, quiet calm of Millet's workers, however, and instead is an unidealistic rendering of a figure slightly stooped from hardship. At the bottom of the work is written, *"La terre, c'est comme les femmes, ça veut être secoué"* (The earth, like women, wants to be shaken). The phrase reflects a typical nineteenth-century sexist viewpoint, relating masculinity with active power and femininity with a passive sexuality.

J.A.B.

# JEAN FRANÇOIS MILLET (1814–75)

François Millet, who had earlier lived in a changing and increasingly more industrialized Paris, was a resident of the rural village of Barbizon when he made his single-figure studies of the 1850s and '60s. These paintings offer a romantic interpretation of the simplicity and nobility of the peasant life, and of its proximity to the natural world. Millet's view of this life was born of emerging French nationalism and the nineteenth-century struggle to maintain individual freedom in a changing political and social structure.

The *Code Napoléon*, of 1808, helped to abolish the distinction between peasantry and nobility in that it specified that no perpetual or irredeemable obligations could be imposed on the basis of ownership of land. The code helped to eliminate the servitude of sharecropping and the enslaving poverty consequent to it, and, radically, declared the freedom of the individual and equality before the law. The number of small, privately owned farms in France increased throughout the nineteenth century, which improved the rural standard of living.

But even as private ownership increased, the daily life of the peasants was brutal. Work occupied seventeen to eighteen hours a day; diet was at best vegetarian, and rarely varied from soup and bread. In the poorest regions, fuel was in such short supply that bread was baked once a year and soaked in salt water to preserve it. Protein was rarely part of the diet; farmers in those regions that produced dairy foods often sold them rather than consuming them. Farming methods remained primitive, for there was little money with which to make technical improvements, even where they were available. However, with the building of roads and, from 1860 onwards, of railroads, rural isolation cracked: national markets were connected, differentiation of production within regions could begin, alternative crops and industries (winemaking, timbering, mining) began to be profitable, and a massive immigration from rural to urban areas began.

Against this background, Millet's studies of peasants bespeak a calm, methodical approach to life in a benign natural world. One almost senses the repetitive motion of the rake or sickle, or of the sower's hand, in this culture of hand labor.

Millet owed some of his inspiration to eighteenth-century French painting—particularly the work of Chardin, whose figures, often in profile, were also involved with work. But Millet's interpretation showed a greater monumentality of the figure within the picture composition. His women especially are more solid, more coarse in their facial features, isolated in work rather than part of a detailed domestic interior. These figures are archetypes—faceless symbols of the common people.

The background of *Peasant Woman Raking* shows Millet's habitual bright palette, abstracted areas of color, and interest in light, which prefigured the Impressionist painting of the next decade.

Millet's work was popular with Boston collectors during the last twenty years of the nineteenth century; many Bostonians studied in France during the 1850s, most notably William Morris Hunt, who brought the influence of Millet and the Barbizon School home to an intellectual society influenced by Emerson, Thoreau, and Whitman, and already quick to find moral overtones in nature.

J.A.B.

## BIBLIOGRAPHY

Weber, Eugen. *Peasants into Frenchmen: The Modernization of Rural France, 1870–1914.* Stanford: Stanford University Press, 1976.

Murphy, Alexandra R. *Jean François Millet.* Boston: Museum of Fine Arts, 1984.

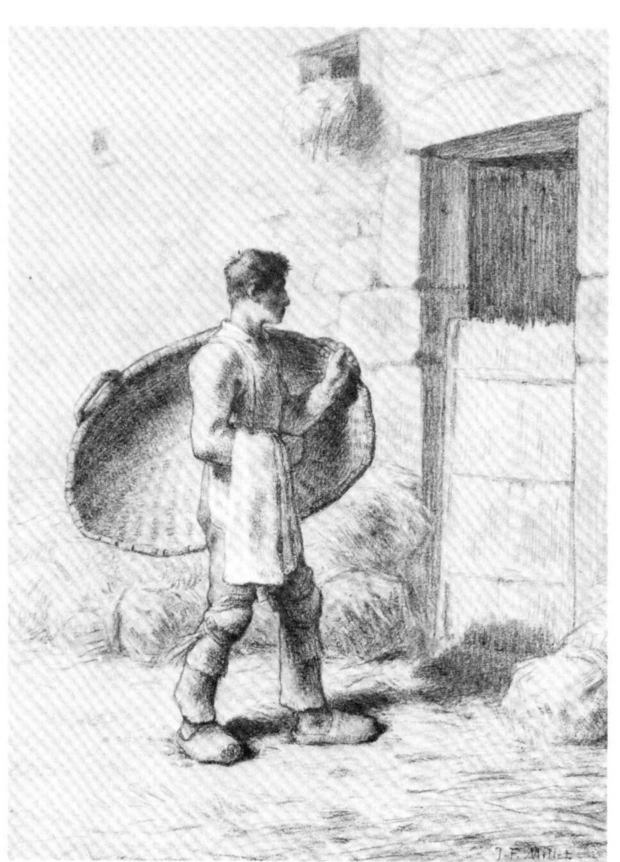

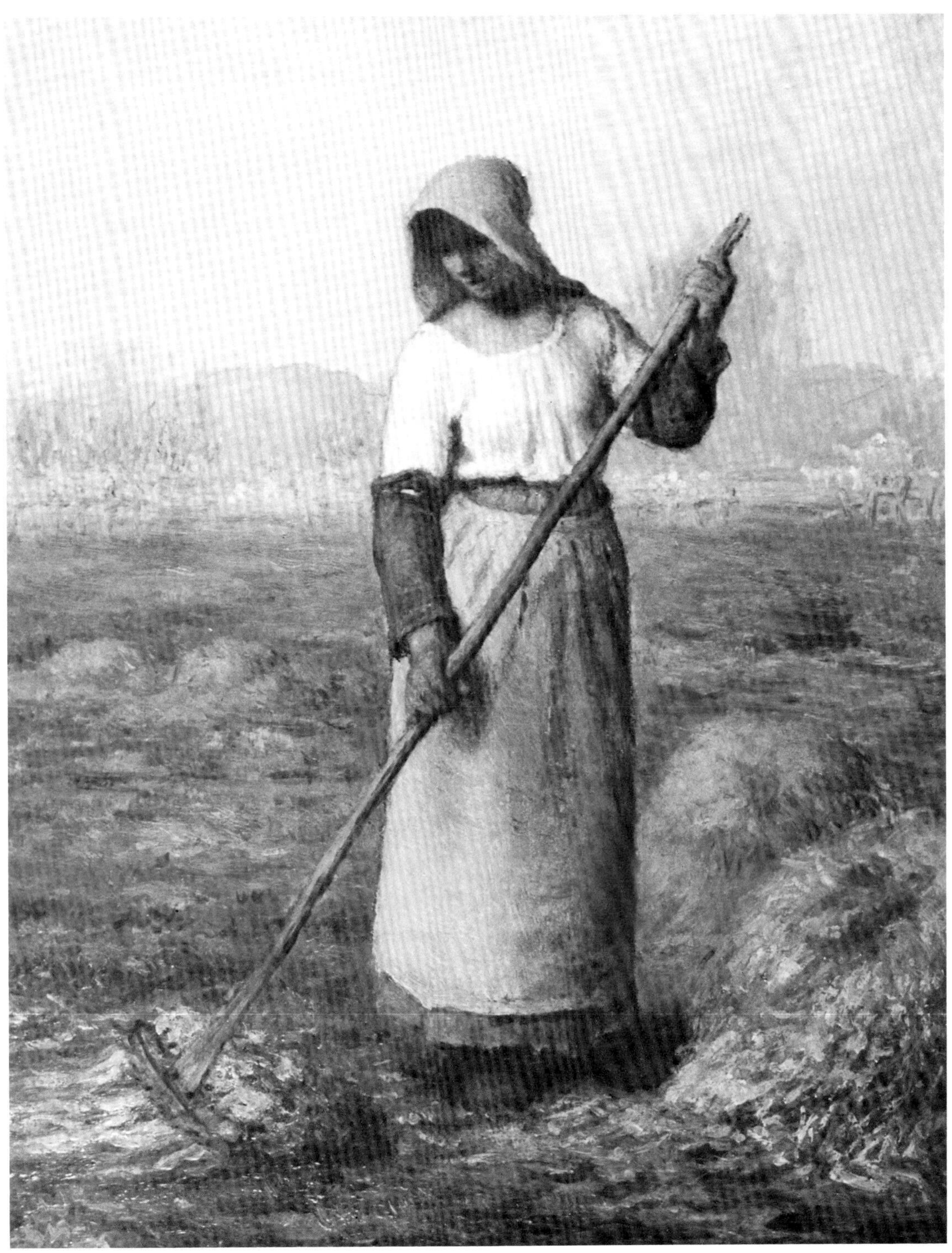

*Peasant Woman Raking*, c. 1855–60
Oil on panel
13⅛ x 10¼ ″
Gift of Mrs. John Simpson and Miss Jean Simpson
1942.86


*Man Holding a Winnowing Basket*, c. 1855–60
Crayon and pencil drawing on gray paper
18 x 12¾ ″
Gift of Charles H. Morgan
1976.99

## HENRI JOSEPH HARPIGNIES (1819–1916)

Certain artists attain undisputed mastery in their given métier, and their reputations are sustained over the years, but they nevertheless receive little mention in art-historical accounts. Their fate of undeserved neglect is not due to any lack of creative achievement, but rather to a life of independent effort that places them apart from the trends and schools of their time. Characteristically, they are without conspicuous predecessors, and equally they are apt to lack either students or historical issue. One such person is the nineteenth-century French painter Henri Joseph Harpignies. His talent flowered late, and in virtual isolation from the main currents of his time. He remained aloof from the complex artistic issues of his day, seeking allegiance with neither classicist, Romantic, nor realist factions.

One of the few artists of rank whom Harpignies got to know well was Corot, whose works were to him almost synonymous with an Italy he visited only twice—and the first time somewhat briefly. Indeed, Harpignies's works do not really resemble Corot's, for all the esteem in which he held that artist and his work, except in one crucial respect: from Corot, Harpignies seems to have learned the essential significance of the classical grid, which locks each of his compositions into a whole. Harpignies is sometimes associated with the Barbizon group, yet he was not acquainted with any artists of that school save for Constant Troyon (1810–65), whom he met once and in passing as a youth. He always treasured a few words of casual encouragement from Troyon upon one of his early showings of his work. Like Corot, Harpignies traveled widely in France, and loved to paint its varied landscape. But aside from his basically realist persuasion—one wholly in tune with the era in which he lived—he worked in splendid solitude. For all that, he was honored in contemporary opinion, and has been survived by a modest but sustained reputation.

Harpignies arrived at his commitment to becoming a professional painter rather late, at age twenty-seven. The son of a prosperous processor of beet sugar, he was put to work in the family refinery after pursuing formal schooling that was, to judge by his own accounts, mediocre enough. Thanks to the intervention of a friend of his father's who had served as his intellectual mentor, in 1846 the young man was finally permitted to study painting under a minor artist of his acquaintance, Jean-Alexis Achard (1807–84). His childhood interest in drawing then began to take shape.

Study in Paris, begun shortly before the revolution of 1848, was interrupted when he sought safer circumstances in Belgium.

By 1850, Harpignies's father had agreed to finance the first of his two trips to Italy. Curiously, his journal of the period lacks mention of museums, papal pomp, or whatever: there is much talk, however, of his involvement with music at the Académie Française in Rome. (He played the cello.) By 1853 he had begun to exhibit in Paris; by 1861 he had attracted notice in the prestigious *Gazette des beaux arts*. But it was not until 1883 that he became associated with a Paris dealer (the major firm of Arnold and Tripp). He was then sixty-four years of age, but at last hitting the stride that would persist throughout three decades yet to come. He won official decorations. He traveled throughout France, and in later years frequented the picturesque towns of the Côte d'Azur, particularly Mentôn. Although he taught his craft passingly as an older man, he left no school—only the example of his work.

The canvas recently acquired for the Mead Art Museum shows Harpignies at his mature best, as an artist of simple tastes who loved the tree rather than the forest, as his biographer, Léonce Bénédite, well observed. In oils and watercolors, both equally admirable, he painted with a vigor and freshness of touch readily mistaken as the signs of a much younger artist's hand. Only in his landscape drawings does his lifelong affection for the qualities of the surface in Corot's work come through in an obvious way, as may be seen in two fine late studies by Harpignies also in the Amherst College Collection. Otherwise, to judge from his works in color, he might almost be taken for an Impressionist. But Harpignies's affection for the glow of earth forms seen under bright blue skies had nothing to do with Impressionist theories. Once again, it is with the traditional structural probity of Corot, not with the looser improvisations of the Impressionists, that he is to be more readily associated. Comparisons aside, however, the art of Harpignies is best appreciated in its own terms, as described by his admirer Bénédite. In what was in effect his valedictory pronouncement, published in the *Gazette des beaux arts* in 1917, the year after the artist's death, Bénédite praises Harpignies's art as "robust, sane and virile, lacking any pretension." He concludes that it is a hymn to the tranquil and majestic triumph of an eternal nature. That is no small recommendation of it to the fresh attention of our own age.

F.T.

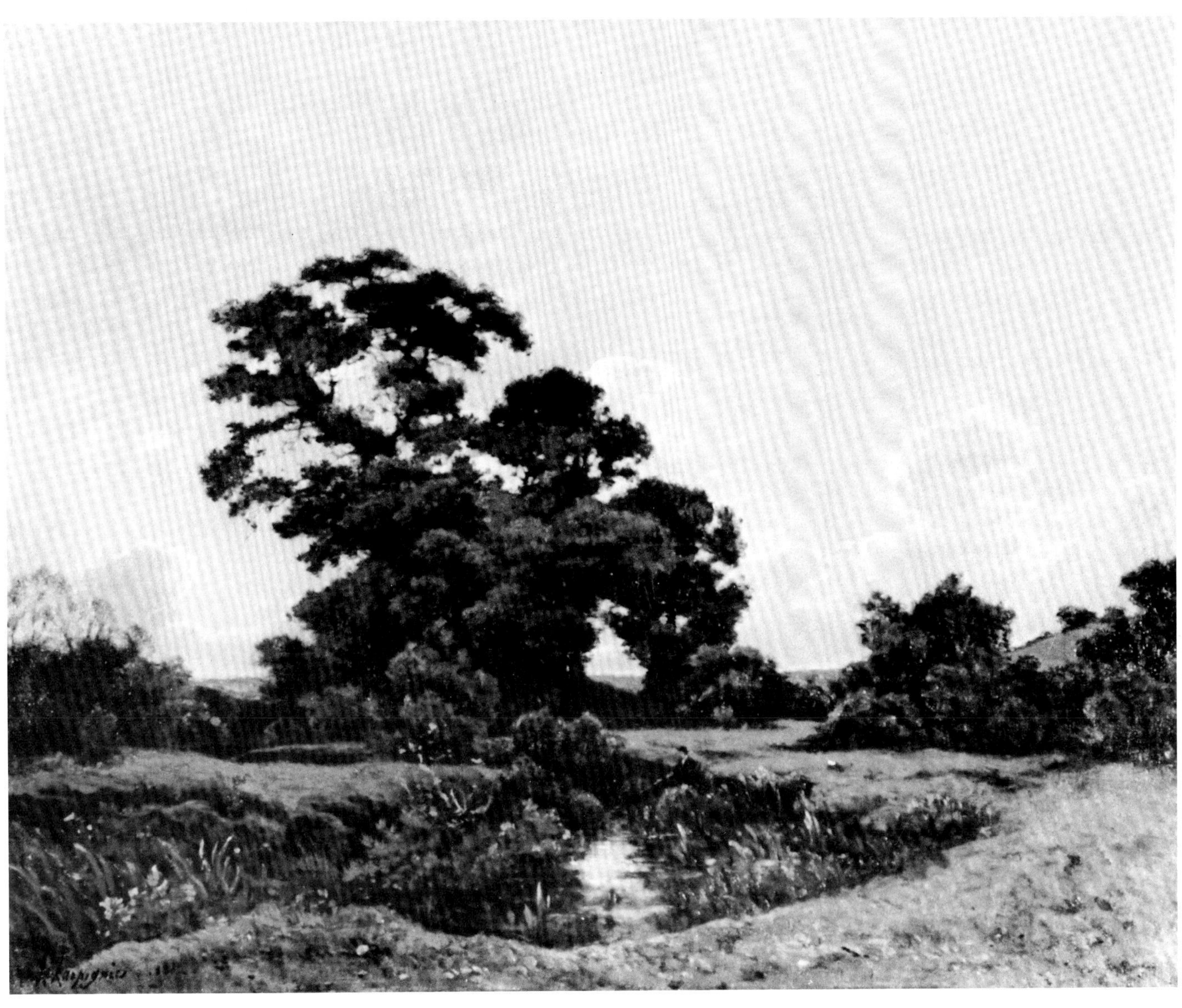

*Paysage au pêcheur au bord du Loing,* 1882
Oil on canvas
21⅝ x 25⅝'
Museum purchase
1987.6

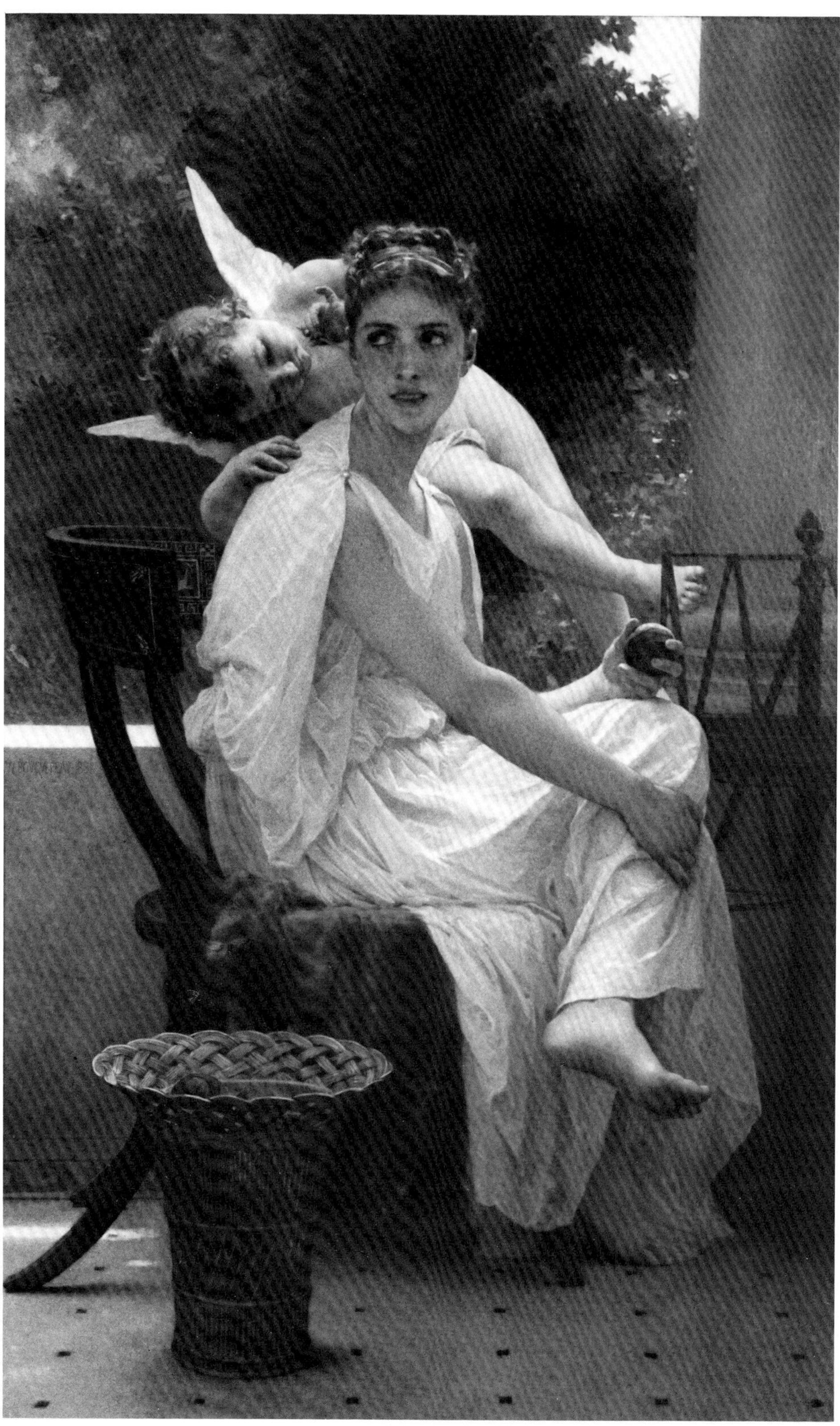

*Le Travail interrompu (Penelope)*, 1891
Oil on canvas
63 x 39¼ ″
Museum purchase
1971.54

# ADOLPHE WILLIAM BOUGUEREAU
## (1825–1905)

The persistence of Neoclassical themes inspired by Greek and Roman literature continued in nineteenth-century academic painting despite the emergence of the Impressionist and Post-Impressionist movements. But Adolphe William Bouguereau's official, academic classicism lacks the moral earnestness or didactic purpose of the neoclassical movement of a century earlier. Unlike early classical subjects by Jacques-Louis David, whose idealized figures dramatize episodes from Greek and Roman history, Bouguereau's classical subjects have the aspect of the *tableau vivant* about them—they are more staged and sensual in feeling, and lack the more authoritative nobility and hardness of style of the late eighteenth century.

Bouguereau, who studied at the Académie Française in Rome from 1850 to '54 was immersed in Renaissance art and upheld the classicizing style in the face of great change in French painting. He was never influenced by the realism of his contemporaries Courbet or Manet, nor by the eroticism of the figural compositions of Auguste Renoir or the geometry of Paul Cézanne.

This picture has been variously titled *Le Travail interrompu* (Interrupted Labor), *Playful Cupid*, and, later, *Penelope.* The title *Penelope* refers to the wife of Odysseus, who spent her days weaving tapestry and hoping for her husband's return from the Trojan War. Pursued by suitors, she agreed to pick a new husband from among them when she had finished her tapestry, but, at night, she secretly unraveled each day's weaving to prevent the fulfillment of her promise. While eighteenth-century Neoclassical painters viewed the loyal Penelope as a figure of virtue and stoicism, Bouguereau's Penelope (if she is indeed the subject here) is a woman distracted by Cupid and thoughts of love—young, vibrant, sensuous, tempted.

J.A.B.

## REFERENCES

*William Bouguereau*, exhibition catalog (Montreal: Le Musée des Beaux-Arts de Montréal, 1984).

Robert Rosenblum and M. W. Janson, *Nineteenth-Century Art* (New York: Harry N. Abrams, 1984).

# CLAUDE MONET (1840–1926)

Claude Monet settled in the village of Giverny in 1883, and despite periods of work elsewhere—in Normandy, Norway, or the French Riviera, in London or Venice—he maintained roots there until his death, in 1926. At Giverny he established his own small paradise, the lily pond and garden that would serve as a constant source of inspiration for most of the canvases of his later years. By this point in his career, Monet had modified his aims and practices of former times. The characteristic Impressionist emphasis on intensely colorful, objectively inclined description progressively gave way to an emphasis on lyrical, chromatic visions, normally pursued outdoors but, as in the case of the "Water Lilies" series of the last years, completed in his spacious studio. His motifs, once chosen somewhat spontaneously, assumed deliberately serial relationships, in which the play of tonal harmonies became as important as the inspiration of season or time of day. Whether in his monumental visions of the façade of Rouen Cathedral, painted in 1893, or in the still more elusively defined natural shapes he rendered in his garden or in the neighboring landscape around Giverny, he devoted himself to the purification of his art.

A crucial stage of that process of redefinition is to be appreciated in a series of Monet's views of the banks of the River Epte, which joins the Seine not far from the painter's home. A visitor to the master reported that by August of 1897 there were fourteen canvases, all begun "at the same time, a range of studies of the same motif, each one modified by the hour, the sun, and the clouds."[1] By 1898, eighteen versions of the subject were completed, for exhibition as a group. At the time, small islands were still to be seen at the confluence of the Epte and the Seine. (Subsequent dredging of the channels has drastically altered the character of those parts, and the islands have disappeared.) Off one of them, the Île aux Orties, Monet had anchored a barge to serve as a temporary studio. His regimen was demanding. He departed cross-country and by small boat to his floating vantage point, so that he could observe the mists that still gather there at dawn and dusk. His depictions of that situation capture not only the visual qualities of atmosphere and light to be experienced there, but also something of the quiet of such a place, at once absorptive of noises yet alive with the awakening sounds of the dawning day.

The Mead picture is one of the finest products of that particular campaign, which marked a crucial step in Monet's thematic and technical development, for it was at that very point that he was planning his most daring and monumental conceptions, the series of paintings of water lilies. Those even-more-radical departures from the original, now "classic" notions of Impressionism would woo the painter from his staunch adherence to working outdoors, *en plein air*, to pursue much of the task of refining his vast, panoramic canvases indoors, in the new studio he would build on his property in 1899. He would, of course, continue to work outdoors in his garden, often with great boldness and dash. But the evocative series showing mornings on the Seine retains a special place in his development, as the example now at Mead reassures us.

F.T.

1. See Daniel Wildenstein, "Monet's Giverny," *Monet's Years at Giverny*, exhibition catalog (New York: Metropolitan Museum of Art, 1978), p. 24.

*Morning on the Seine, Giverny,* from the series
    "Matinées sur la Seine," 1897
Oil on canvas
31½ x 35½"
Bequest of Miss Susan Dwight Bliss
1966.48

## HENRI DE TOULOUSE-LAUTREC
(1864–1901)

This early masterwork by Henri de Toulouse-Lautrec portrays the artist's father, the eccentric Count Alphonse de Toulouse-Lautrec, at the age of forty-five. Given more to the pleasures of blood sports, especially falconry, than to parenthood and husbandry, the count is shown, appropriately enough, on horseback. Ironically, his son Henri, the young scion of an aristocratic heritage that traced its lineage directly back to Charlemagne, suffered a pair of crippling riding accidents, which left him deformed and increasingly alienated from the world of privilege into which he had been born. Henri's love of horseflesh, shown here in an early guise, would nevertheless continue to manifest itself in spirited later subjects stimulated by his love of the racetrack and circus.

Still barely twenty years of age at the time he undertook this portrait of his father, Toulouse-Lautrec tests his mettle in a large and vigorously handled *ébauche*, or unfinished piece. His later technical predilections are already conspicuous, particularly in the use of thin washes of oil color, applied with unhesitating spontaneity. Another forecast of Toulouse-Lautrec's developed manner is his bold, calligraphic use of a line capable of suggesting the whole of an image with a synoptic clarity. At times, as here, he almost willfully abandoned his subject, making tantalizing suggestions of potential adjustments or corrections that would never take shape. At this budding of his artistry Toulouse-Lautrec shows in particular the value of lessons learned under the tutelage of René Princeteau (1844?–1914), whose spirited equestrian subjects offered accomplished models to emulate. But in this remarkable effort by the pupil there already lurks a note of the powerful, often disquieting energy that would remain characteristic of his mature works, traits that play no role in the repertory of his fashionable mentor.

F.T.

*Count de Toulouse-Lautrec on Horseback*
(Le Comte Alphonse de Toulouse-Lautrec), 1883
Oil on canvas
36¾ x 25⅝″
Gift of Harold F. Johnson, '18
1953.64

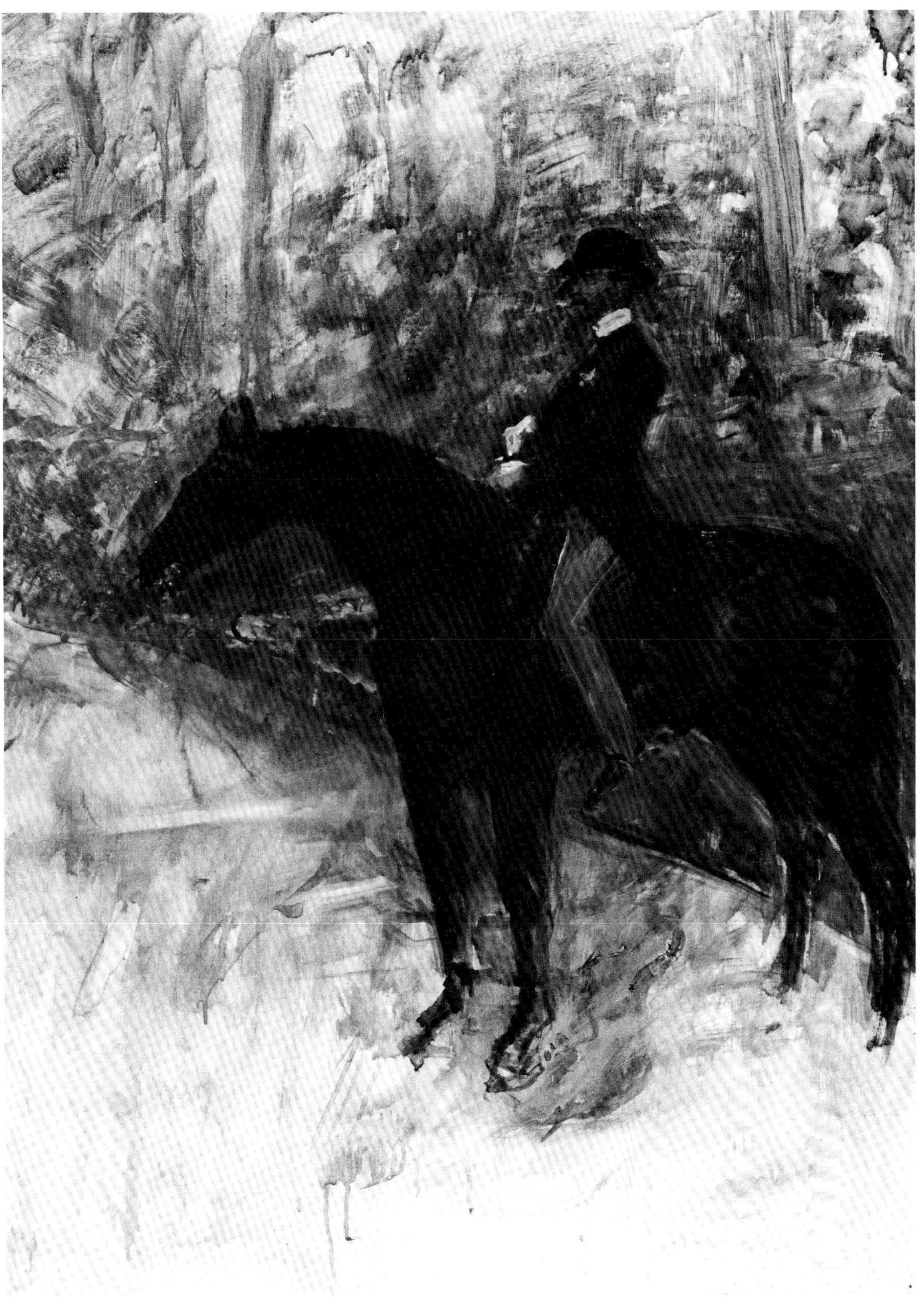

## GUSTAVE LOISEAU (1865–1935)

Although he was directly associated with the Symbolist or Synthetist movement centered at Pont-Aven in Brittany, and although he came to share many of the ideas fostered in the coterie that formed there around Paul Gauguin, Gustave Loiseau maintained fundamental allegiances to the parent practices of Impressionism. A modest man, lacking the ambitiousness (and some of the pretensions) of his fellows among the Gauguin following, he nevertheless responded to the aesthetic and moral speculations that animated the exchanges of that group. From 1890 onward, Loiseau was a member of the small colony of avant-garde artists who continued to gather in Brittany during the summers, even after Gauguin himself had gone farther afield in his search for artistic and personal truths.

While it has been said that Loiseau's work is close in style to Monet's, *The Cliffs of Saint Jouin* actually resembles more closely the soft and feathery manner of Renoir. Loiseau's color harmonies as well seem more related to the particular sparkle of Renoir's canvases, with their heightened artifice of palette. Perhaps this trait marks Loiseau's affinities with Symbolist doctrines, with their belief in the expressive virtues of intensified coloration for creating decorative and ''symbolic'' pictorial effects. Whatever the case, the present composition was painted in the years when Loiseau's exposure to the Symbolist doctrines was still recent, and his artistic responses to them were admirably fresh and vigorous.

F.T.

*Les Falaises de Saint Jouin*, 1908
Oil on canvas
23½ x 32″
Gift of Mrs. Margaret E. French, in memory of her
    husband, Paul C. French, '26
1985.41

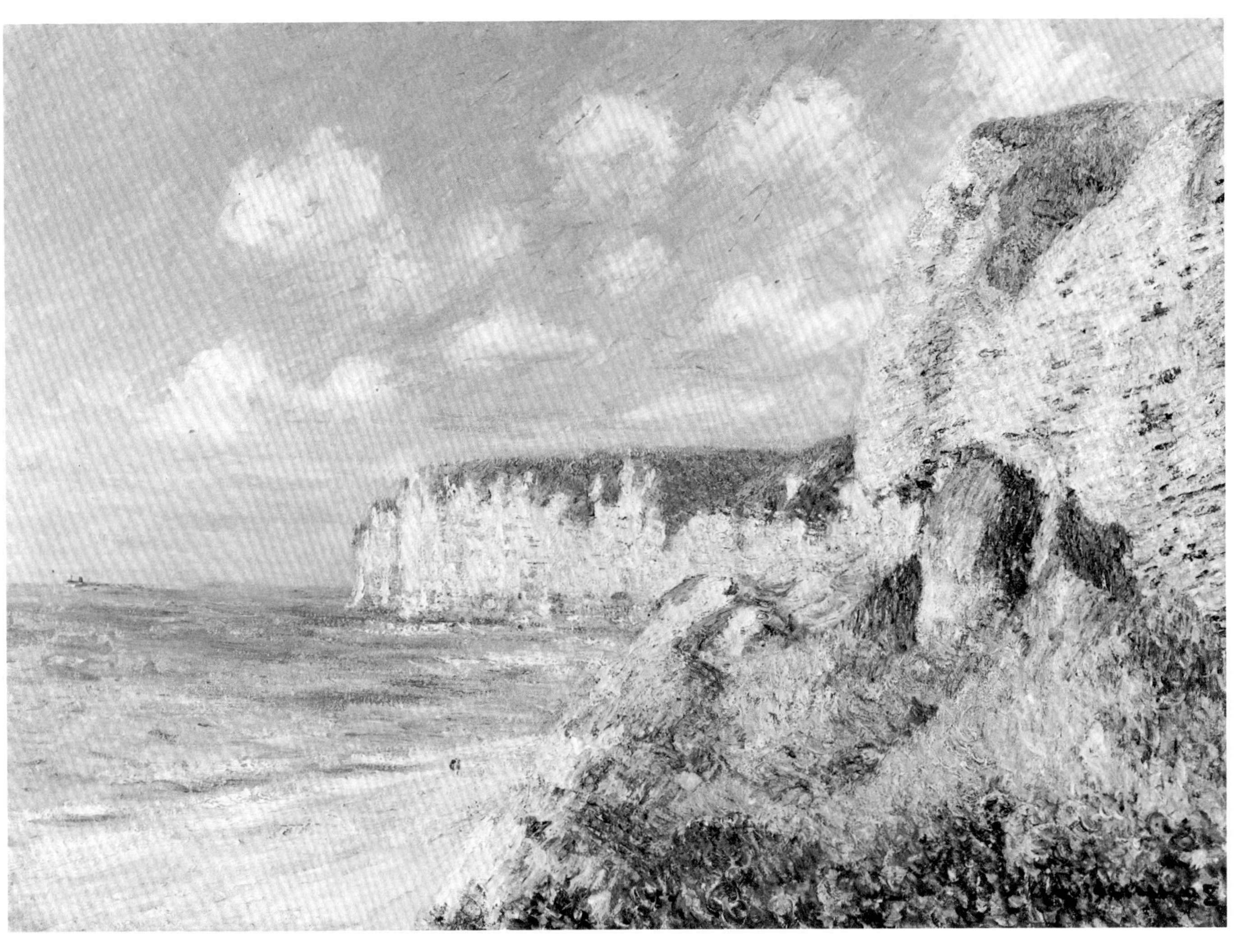

# Nineteenth-Century French Prints from the Collection of Edward C. Crossett

JAY M. FISHER

The print collection of the Mead Art Museum provides students and other museum visitors with a comprehensive survey of the history of graphic art. Within that survey, the greatest depth lies in the nineteenth-century French holdings. The scope and character of Mead's collection in this area is owed mainly to the interests of Edward C. Crossett, who in 1951 bequeathed to Amherst College the principal part of the collection he had formed in the years before World War II. Since that time, the Museum staff has knowledgeably encouraged further donations and made purchases to strengthen the collection as a teaching instrument in the educational program of the College.

Although Crossett left no written explanation of his collecting interests, or of the strategy he used in building his collection, his orientation as a collector may be deduced from the objects themselves. it should be noted, however, that parts of the Crossett Collection were dispersed to other recipients, so it is not possible to reconstruct the collection just as Crossett left it. The Amherst bequest is primarily limited to etchings, with comparatively few examples of lithography, the other major printmaking medium in nineteenth-century France. For the most part, the Museum's excellent holdings of early French lithography from the Romantic era, some of which are discussed elsewhere in this monograph, were acquired after the Crossett bequest, as also were numerous examples of turn-of-the-century color lithographs by Henri de Toulouse-Lautrec, Édouard Vuillard, Pierre Bonnard, and others. Crossett himself was attracted to artists who were known primarily as printmakers, rather than to the experimental printmaking of those who were chiefly active as painters, like Camille Pissarro. Notable exceptions to

this bias would be Crossett's fine examples of prints by Jean-Auguste Dominique Ingres, Édouard Manet, and Edgar Degas.

In addition, Crossett collected few artists in depth, aside from the Barbizon master Charles Daubigny and the later etcher and wood-engraver Auguste Lepère. Most of Crossett's prints could readily have come from American dealers who specialized in French etchings of this period, for there is little evidence of surprising discoveries among his selections. In that sense, the collection can fairly be called predictable, as the objects chosen were among the most popular and, therefore, the most readily available at the time Crossett was collecting. Reflecting the actual history of the etching medium in the nineteenth century, landscapes and city views predominate as subjects.

The taste Crossett shared for collecting etchings was guided by a kind of connoisseurship that seeks the special proof, the unusual printing, or the rare intermediate state. Predispositions of the sort did not transfer easily to the different aesthetic of the lithograph. At a time when many contemporary artists had moved far from the pastoral realism of the mid century, many American collectors remained intensely interested in French and English etchings, which were still being produced in that earlier style. Crossett, however, concentrated primarily on the nineteenth-century masters rather than on their twentieth-century followers. For example, he sought out a choice early Neoclassical work by Ingres and fine examples of the opposing Romanticism of Eugène Delacroix. He represented the Barbizon School through Daubigny and the mid-century technicians, through Félix Bracquemond and Maxime Lalanne. Finally, he included more experimental and original applications of the medium in prints by Félix Buhot, Mary Cassatt, and Degas.

To restrict a collection of nineteenth-century prints mainly to etchings is not as narrow a focus as it may at first seem. Until the 1890s, etching predominated as a medium of preference. Lithography, invented late in the preceding century, soon fell from favor, while engraving was stigmatized as the province of overly academic reproductive engravers. The discussions on the artistic merit of printmaking carried on by such critics as Charles Baudelaire and Théophile Gautier centered on a so-called "etching revival" in the 1860s.

Apparently Crossett was systematic in building his collection, seeking accessible prints at modest prices.

His impressions are well chosen and individualized, rather than standard-edition printings. Today, collectors with a similar goal would have a considerably larger bibliography to advise them. In the last two decades, a wide range of publications has broadened our knowledge of French printmaking of Crossett's preferred era. Well-known artists have been thoroughly catalogued, and lesser known figures rescued from the vagaries of taste. When Crossett was collecting, he had to rely primarily on the word of dealers and on the authority of a group of relatively superficial surveys written without benefit of primary research. These documents represented, moreover, a distillation of the opinions of an epoch just past, without the benefit of the revisions of view that the passage of time encourages.

Not surprisingly, the surveys concentrated primarily on the art of etching, which could readily be described with reference to a continuum of historical precedents. And since collectors were their principal readers, it is not surprising that the marketplace had much to do with both the surveys' selection of artists and their adoption of an overly technical approach to the printmaker's art. Hence the experimental trials of an artist like Pissarro, which because of rarity and lack of promotion gained little attention from collectors, were compared with the products of more popular etchers such as Buhot. Though smaller, the Crossett Collection is not unlike the great collections of French prints of the period built by Samuel Avery for the New York Public Library, or by George Lucas in Baltimore, since collectors in the early twentieth century tended to perpetuate what had been popular several decades before. While the Mead collection is adequately cataloged, it is not well known, and deserves more consideration as another important resource for the study of nineteenth-century art.

The earliest nineteenth-century etching in the Crossett Collection is the distinctive *Portrait of Cardinal Gabriel Cortois de Pressigny*, executed by Ingres (1780–1867) in 1816 (fig. 1). The artist's only known etching, it closely follows the drawing style of his distinctive pencil portraits. Inasmuch as this print is in fact a copy by Ingres of his drawing of the cardinal, now in a private Paris collection, its virtue lies not in its originality of conception but in its testimony to the

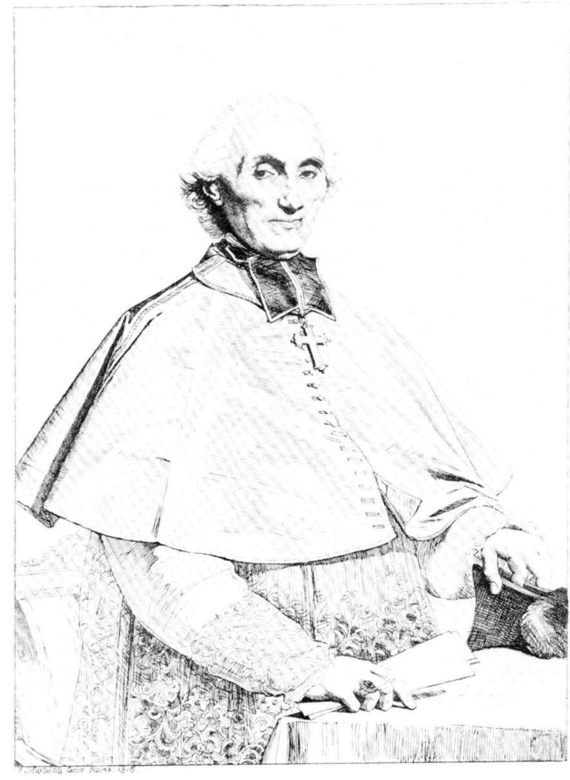

Fig. 1

Jean-Auguste Dominique Ingres (1780–1867)
*Cardinal Gabriel Cortois de Pressigny*, 1816
Etching, 3rd state of 3 12½ x 8¾ ″
Gift of Edward C. Crossett, '05
1951.1249

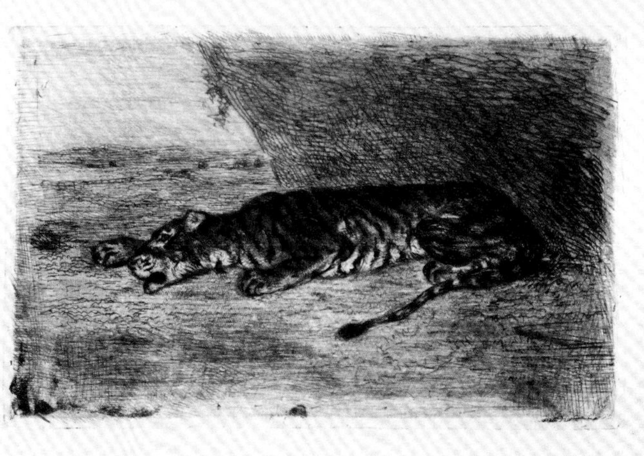

Fig. 2

Ferdinand Victor Eugène Delacroix (1798–1863)
*Tigre couché à l'entrée de son antre*, 1829
Etching, 5th state of 6, 3¾ x 5⅝′
Gift of Edward C. Crossett, '05
1951.970

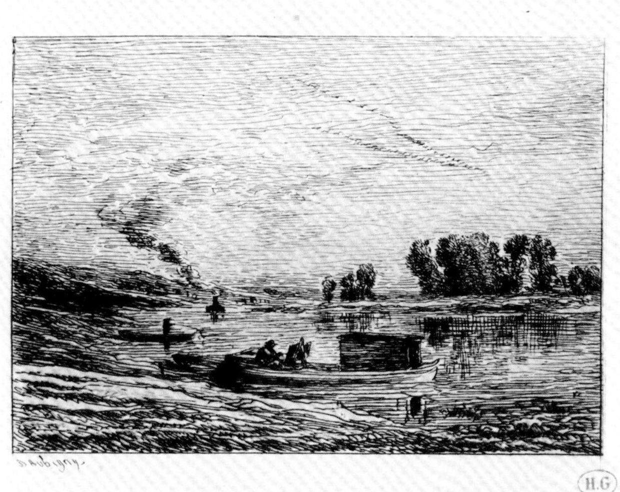

Fig. 3

Charles François Daubigny (1817–78)
*Le Paysagiste en bateau*, 1866
Etching, 1st state of 3, 4½ x 5⅝"
Gift of Edward C. Crossett, '05
1951.879

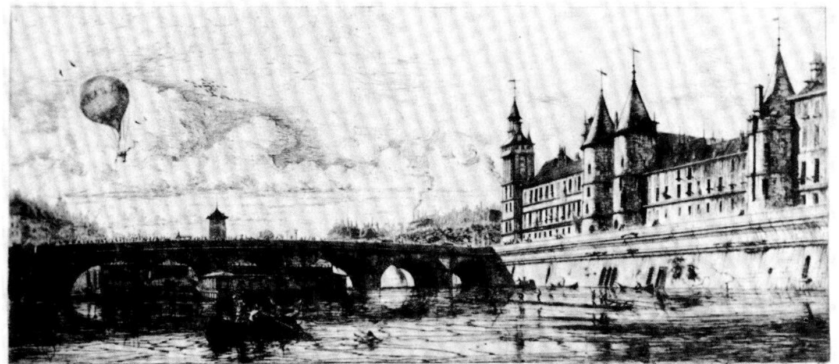

Fig. 4

Charles Meryon (1821–68)
*Le Pont-au-Change*, 1854
Etching, 5th state of 11, 6⅛ x 13"
Gift of Edward C. Crossett, '05
1951.1772

artist's ability to capture in a print the effect of silvery pencil lines, clear yet luminous. Because of its early date, this etching is often cited as a precedent for increased interest in that medium in subsequent decades. Ingres's artistic model was the seventeenth-century portrait-etching manner of Anthony van Dyck, with the costume detail rapidly drawn and the face realized in more detail. On the other hand, the starkly linear effect of the piece must surely be the result of influence from the line engravings so basic to the eighteenth-century academic training. In the hands of common professional engravers, this style produced the lifeless mechanical prints decried by protagonists of etching, but Ingres was here able to achieve an etching full of his genius of draftsmanship. Even though this portrait of Pressigny should be admired as an original artistic contribution to printmaking, the art etching held little intrinsic interest for Ingres, so he left the subsequent reproduction of his portrait drawings to professional lithographers.

A deeper well of printmaking originality is found in the etchings of Romantic artists, of which the Mead holds a number of fine examples. The most important representative of the group, Delacroix, is included, as also are Alexandre Decamps, Théodore Chassériau, and the landscapist Paul Huet. Most of these artists were equally interested in lithography, as both processes allow unconstrained drawing, which is carried through directly to the printed images, to make them, in fact, multiple drawings. In his small etching *Tiger Sleeping at the Entrance of His Den*, 1829 (fig. 2), Delacroix drew rapidly, without concern for scientific description. He sought instead to communicate the almost human character of a beast undoubtedly observed in a zoo, although here situated in a desert. Only a few of Delacroix's thirty-five etchings were published during his lifetime, as widespread appreciation for his printmaking was postponed until shortly after his death, in 1863, when the commercial market for etching was greater and collectors were eager to include such an early advocate of the medium in their collections.

Published at about the same time were the landscape etchings made by Huet (1803–69) from the 1830s onward. Huet found his precedents in the landscapes etched by seventeenth-century Dutch artists. Whether depicting actual scenes or imaginary forest and marine views, Huet's landscapes are animated by a vibrant nature.

In the 1840s the Barbizon painters worked out-of-doors, to capture a quieter, less romantic view of nature. They too were satisfied by the etching medium, which allowed them to render spontaneously the landscape in which they were working. Crossett liked these artists, especially Charles Daubigny (1817–78), for he collected some thirty-odd of his prints. In Daubigny's etching *The Landscapist in a Boat*, 1866 (fig. 3), part of his series "Voyage en bateau," the artist is shown in his floating studio, from which he could observe intimately the life and landscape along the river. He probably did not carry prepared copper plates with him, but used his drawings later to prepare the series of etchings for publication as a group. Daubigny and Charles Émile Jacque, also represented in the Crossett Collection, were the most prolific nineteenth-century etchers; each of them etched hundreds of plates. Both were enormously influential in the evolution of the medium, and they greatly popularized the landscape as an appropriate subject matter for etchers, which it remained until the early twentieth century. Prints by these early Barbizon artists were characteristically published in editions, and were often included in such periodicals as *L'Artiste*, the major vehicle for the distribution of original etchings in the first half of the nineteenth century.

By the 1850s, artists had begun to explore a wider range of subject matter and to capitalize on the inherent versatility of the medium, with its allowance for a full range of drawing styles, whether rapid and suggestive or precisely descriptive. Notions of landscape were in the process broadened to include the cityscape, especially views of Paris. Charles Meryon (1821–68) was certainly the greatest practitioner of this genre. He explored artistic precedents different from those that had served the Barbizon artists, being particularly attracted to the eighteenth-century Italian architectural etchings of Antonio Canaletto and Giovanni Battista Piranesi. Meryon possessed masterly descriptive powers. His drawing style reveals a careful delineation of architectural detail, with surfaces animated by textural variation. Since he was not a painter, he concentrated wholly on his prints. Unlike his contemporaries, who entrusted their work to professional printers, Meryon printed his plates personally, and was therefore able to add subtle effects to them through interpretive wiping. The Crossett impression of *The Pont-au-Change*, 1854 (fig. 4), is a good example of that approach, which made

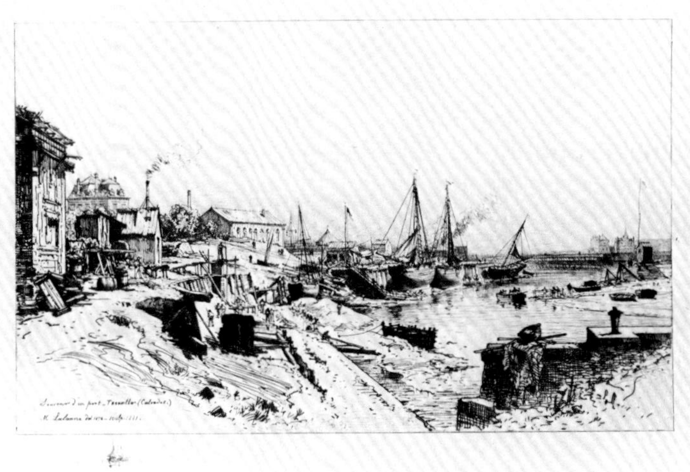

Fig. 5

Maxime François Antoine Lalanne (1827–86)
*Souvenir d'un port—Trouville (Calvados)*
Etching, 10 x 5 ¾ "
Gift of Edward C. Crossett, '05
1951.1308

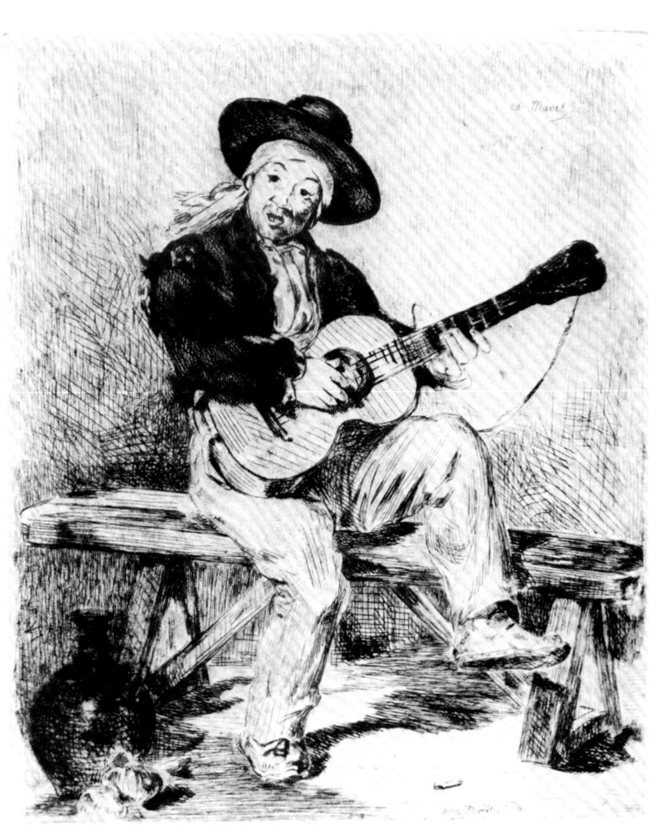

Fig. 6

Édouard Manet (1832–83)
*Le Guitarrero*, 1861
Etching, 11 ¾ x 9 ⅝'
Gift of Edward C. Crossett, '05
1951.1726

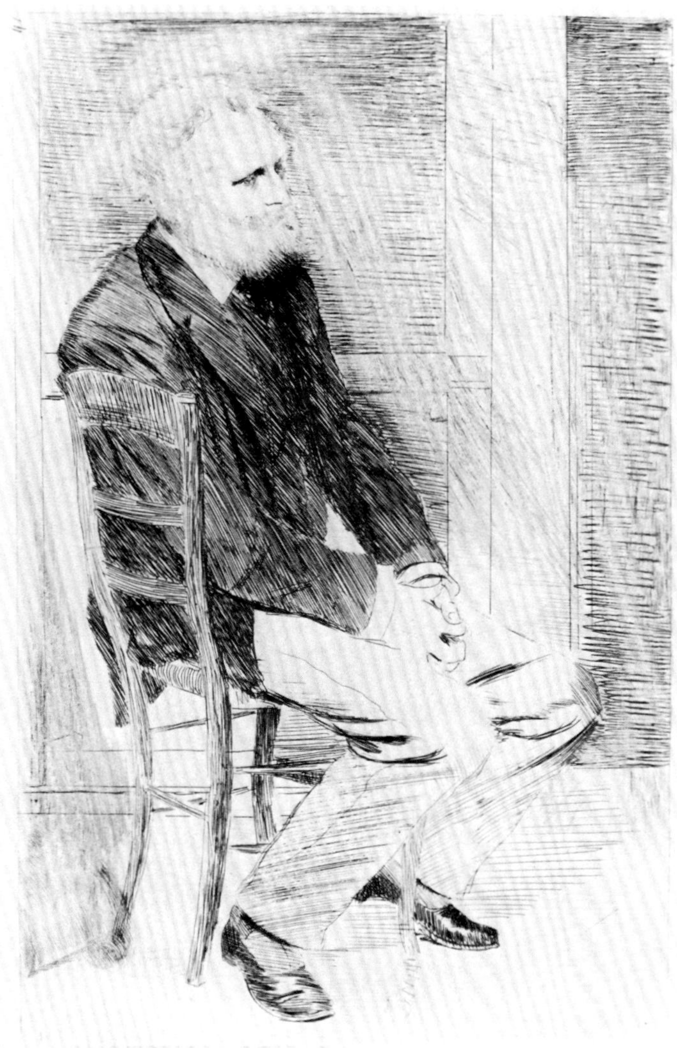

Fig. 7

Hilaire Germain Edgar Degas (1834–1917)
*Manet Seated, Turned to the Right*, 1864
Etching, 4th state of 4, 7½ x 5″
Gift of Edward C. Crossett, '05
1951.950

Fig. 8

Adolphe Appian (1818–98)
*Un Étang près de Rousillon*, 1867
Etching, 9³⁄₁₆ x 6³⁄₈″
Gift of Edward C. Crossett, '05
1951.449

Fig. 9

Johann Barthold Jongkind (1819–91)
*Sortie de la Maison Cochin*, 1878
Etching, 2nd state of 4, 5¾ x 9¼″
Gift of Edward C. Crossett, '05
1951.1277

Meryon's prints popular with collectors desirous of special proofs. Meryon's views of Paris, available separately or in series, were those most in demand. His remarkable descriptive powers aside, Meryon's art was also admired for the vivid imagination it revealed. Familiar Paris scenes were often transformed with bizarre twists of reality.

In 1862 Alfred Cadart, a publisher of prints and books, founded the Société des aquafortistes (Society of Etchers) to capitalize on the growing enthusiasm for etching. He encouraged a number of artists to join the Société as founding members and to produce etchings for periodic portfolios of prints for sale to subscribers. Cadart published etching manuals and sold etching presses and supplies. The Société fostered a number of special exhibitions featuring amateurs as well as more prominent printmakers. These exhibitions provided occasions for major critics such as Baudelaire, Jules Castagnary, and Gautier to write lengthy articles on the virtues of the etching medium, which Cadart then published as introductions to his folios. Baudelaire saw etching as a technique for the "modern" artist, although he cautioned that in revealing the "soul" of the artist, flaws were not easily hidden. There was also a growing market for etchings reproducing paintings, a domain previously reserved for engravers and lithographers. This development did little for the artistic growth of the etching medium, but it did provide commercial support for many artists, helping them to survive.

Maxime Lalanne (1827–86), who wrote Cadart's manual for etchers, represents the pure, somewhat technical approach to etching that prevailed during the years of the Société. For Lalanne, etching was a cause. As early as the late eighteenth century, artists had begun to experiment with various tonal processes, such as aquatint, but Lalanne rejected such variations, believing in the virtue of the pure etched line. *Souvenir d'un port—Trouville (Calvados)* (fig. 5) reveals the technical control that made his work so admired. But far too often Lalanne's prints seem merely expository of his theories. To the Crossett holdings of this period the Mead has since added prints by Félix Bracquemond (1833–1914), who was also a master technician but much more innovative and influential. He encouraged such artists as Manet and Degas to pursue printmaking, and he often gave them technical advice. Bracquemond was also known for introducing Japanese woodcuts to his contemporaries.

The Société lasted only a few years, but was followed by other publishing ventures that ensured a steady market for etchings. Less doctrinaire expectations for the etching medium evolved in the late 1860s and 1870s, and fewer critics singled out etchers for special consideration. Technical purism gave way to experimentation, and a wider variety of approaches emerged. This second generation of etchers emphasized the medium's potential for originality, attempting to separate themselves from its role as a means of mechanical reproduction. The term *peintre-graveurs* (painter-printmakers) was attached to these artists, not because they all were in fact painters (though many were), but because they were eager to identify the creative aspects of their work, by identifying etching more intimately with painting and drawing. In the 1880s attitudes toward lithography underwent a similar transformation, with the medium's release from the context of commercial usage.

Edouard Manet (1832–83) took up the etching needle because he was dissatisfied with the work of the reproductive etchers who made prints after his paintings. At the same time, he sought thereby to distribute his art to a wider public, as well as to enjoy the potential for exploring, in another language, the ideas he had first pursued in painting. Manet's etching *Spanish Singer*, 1861 (fig. 6), is a good example of this, for it reinterprets his well-known canvas to pose a creative dialogue between the two objects. Manet was not a medium-centered artist, and the strength of his etchings arises from the originality of his ideas and their demand for new approaches to each medium.

Much the same can be said for Edgar Degas (1834–1917), whose portrait *Manet Seated, Turned to the Right*, 1864 (fig. 7), is one of several extraordinary Degas prints in the Amherst College Collection. In the case of Degas, Crossett collected lithographs as well as this etching. Like Manet, Degas used printmaking as a way to explore variations of his ideas. Whether in painting, drawing, sculpture, or prints, all his art interrelates. Degas made prints mostly for his own stimulation. They were rarely exhibited or collected during his day. Like Rembrandt's prints, those of Degas are inherently experimental, with their many intermediate stages, constant revisions, and very individualized printing. The Manet portrait is the final state of four in which Degas modified various aspects

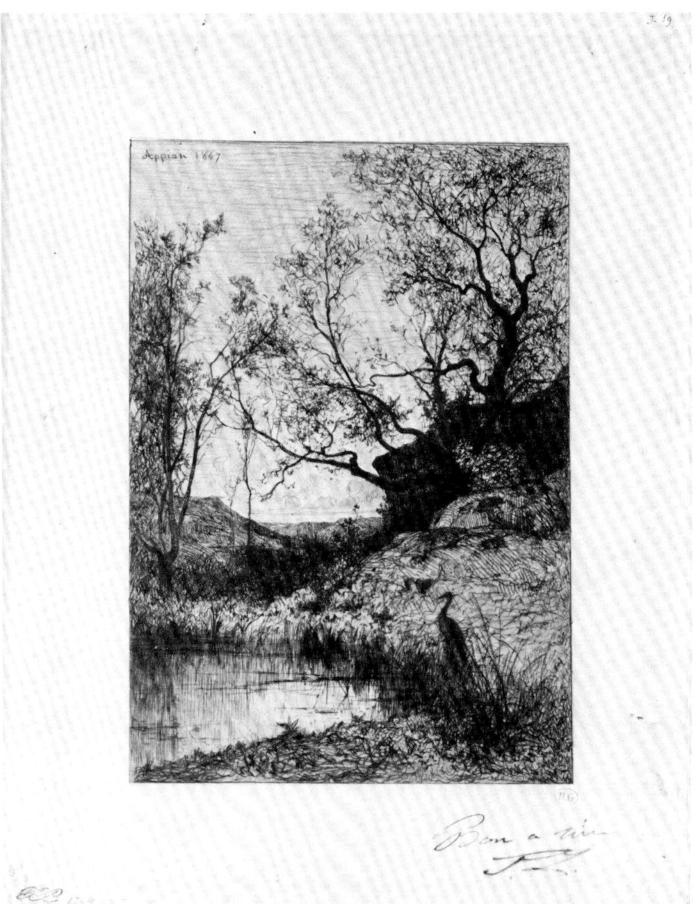

Fig. 8

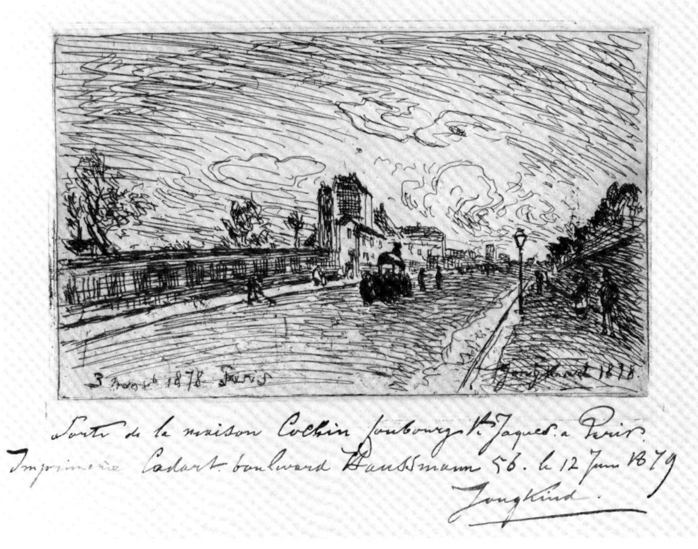

Fig. 9

of the composition, including background, face, and figure. He used all possible combinations of technique, both linear and tonal, in his effort to take what he needed from technical advisers like Bracquemond.

The Crossett Collection contains a very comprehensive representation of the *peintre-graveurs*, including prints by Albert Besnard, Auguste Lepère, Adolphe Appian, Johann Jongkind, and Félix Buhot. These last three are represented by especially fine impressions. Jongkind (1819–91) and Appian (1818–98) concentrated on landscape, while Buhot (1847–98) carried on the work of Meryon with city views of London and Paris. Unlike the more sterile landscapes of the Société etchers, Appian's reveal an atmospheric approach, achieved through the colorful inking of his plates. *A Pool near Roussillon*, 1867 (fig. 8), is an excellent example of a fine, uniquely interpreted proof. By contrast, Jongkind chose to ink his plates cleanly, so that his lively, suggestive line would read clearly against the white of the paper. *Leaving the Maison Cochin, Faubourg Saint-Jacques*, 1878 (fig. 9), is a fine example of his style, so indebted to the landscapes of Rembrandt. Most of the plate is left bare. The essentials of the landscape are captured with relatively few fluid strokes of the etching needle.

Finally, Buhot in his print *Une Jetée en Angleterre*, 1879 (fig. 10), explores the effect of winter in a scene of a windblown English jetty filled with the drama of a rainy storm. Frequently, Buhot would begin with a painting and then try to capture painterly effects through a wide range of etching techniques. His famous views of Paris and London, some portraying rain and snow, were widely collected, especially by Americans. Each of Buhot's proofs, which he often marked with his special "owl" stamp, were printed differently on a wide range of papers, including vellum. He devised all manner of techniques to achieve the effects he desired. Buhot was also a critic, and he wrote often of the etching medium, defending the more creative work of his contemporaries and contesting the commercial orientation that prevailed in the 1860s.

This brief survey of the Crossett holdings can only hint at the depth of the collection. In the last decade, the nineteenth-century holdings of many American museums have been studied and exhibited with greater regularity. Amherst is fortunate to have such an excellent collection with which to study this extraordinary epoch in the history of printmaking.

## SELECTED BIBLIOGRAPHY


Bailly-Herzberg, Janine. *L'Eau-forte de peintre au dix-neuvième siècle—La Société des aquafortistes.* 1862–1867, 2 vols. Paris: Léonce Laget, 1972.

Fisher, Jay, and Baxter, Colles. *Félix Buhot, Peintre Graveur: Prints, Drawings, and Paintings.* Exhibition catalog, Baltimore: The Baltimore Museum of Art, 1983.

Hamerton, Philip Gilbert. *Etching and Etchers.* Boston: Roberts Brothers, 1878.

Leipnik, F. L. *A History of French Etching from the Sixteenth Century to the Present Day.* New York: Dodd, Mead & Co., 1924.

Melot, Michel. *History of an Art: Prints.* Geneva: Skira, 1981.

Reed, Sue Welch, and Shapiro, Barbara Stern. *Edgar Degas: The Painter as Printmaker.* Exhibition catalog, Boston: Museum of Fine Arts, 1984.

Roger-Marx, Claude. *Graphic Art of the 19th Century.* New York: McGraw-Hill Book Company, 1962.


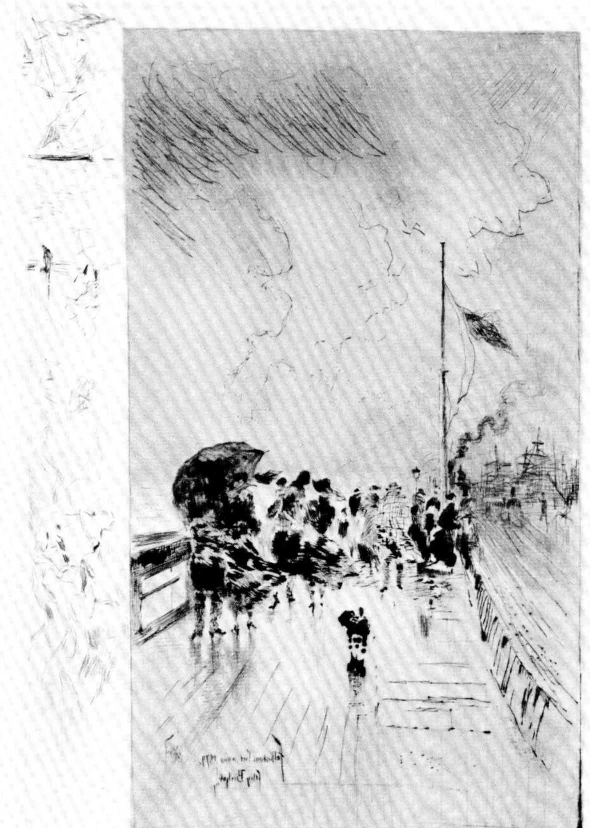

Fig. 10

Félix Buhot (1847–98)
*Une Jetée en Angleterre*, 1879
Etching, 11¾ x 7¾ ″
Gift of Edward C. Crossett, '05
1951.732

# Incunabula of Lithography in France

FRANK TRAPP

Until fairly recent times, the various print mediums were regarded mainly as a cheaper substitute for the uniquely crafted object, even as the printed book was first intended as a more economical substitute for an expensive manuscript. To be sure, distinctions were recognized from the beginning between the preciously wrought work of engraving, with its origins in the art of the jeweler or of the armorer, and the woodcut, born of the humbler crafts of carpentry. Basically, the two graphic forms were originally addressed to different clienteles. The engraving catered to the more affluent, and was conceived as an object to be treasured, like a drawing. The woodcut, even when produced in association with a major master or shop, was generally treated more casually—hence the extreme rarity of some early examples of that art. In either case, the prints produced during the first century of European printmaking, the fifteenth century, are now regarded as ''incunabula''—artifacts from an early period. The term is also applied to works issued during the infancy of the comparatively new lithographic process, in the early nineteenth century, when the lithograph flourished above all in France.

The origins of lithography are not in doubt: the process was invented by a Bavarian actor and dramatist, Aloys Senefelder (1771–1834), who was interested in finding an inexpensive way of publishing his own work. His device, a means of making what were in effect shallow relief engravings in stone, resulted from a series of discoveries in the years 1796–98. He thus launched a new form of printing, which he later published in his *Complete Course of Lithography* (1818). Senefelder's ingenious process was based upon the principle that grease attracts grease and repels water. Thus greasy ink will be retained on crayon or other greasy marks made on stone (or later, on metal), and the marks can then be printed on paper. There are, of course, further stages involved in the actual execution, but the directness and comparative simplicity of lithographic printing was soon recognized by those interested in commercial applications, whether for printing designs on calico or for producing cheap sheet music.

Senefelder's efforts to protect his invention were not wholly successful, and, *faute de mieux*, its use quickly became widespread throughout Europe. In England, lithography was adopted as early as 1801, and credit for its origins was clouded by opportunists. In France, lithographic printing became current slightly later, but with outstanding results, as artists of high distinction explored its promise as a medium of self-expression. Names like Théodore Géricault (1791–1824) and Eugène Delacroix (1798–1863) come especially to mind, along with Francisco Goya (1746–1828), whose ventures into lithography came late in life, after he had taken political exile in Bordeaux.

While plates from Goya's famous lithographic series "Bulls of Bordeaux," are not contained in the Amherst College Collection (although his prints are otherwise outstandingly represented), many other examples of lithography by his younger French contemporaries have been accumulated. Together, they comprise an instructive review of developments in the use of that medium in nineteenth-century France. Here, further introductory notes are in order. Inasmuch as many lithographs are collaborative rather than solo products, the artist's name is duly indicated as the inventor of the original image. Often a collaborator is employed to transfer that image onto the lithographic stone before printing. That second name is also recorded on most impressions. Third, the name of the editor or publisher is also credited in most instances. If rights to the issuance of a plate or series were sold, as was often the case, the publisher's name was changed. In commercial lithographs, the edition thus reflects the order of issuance. Earlier editions are normally more prized for the fresher condition of the image—and often for their rarity as well. When trial proofs (without lettering and sometimes printed on finer paper) turn up, they are understandably of exceptional interest. This is especially so with works by artists like Honoré Daumier, whose prints were published in large editions, often with letterpress texts on the reverse side of the page, which mar the quality of the image. It was only much later that it became customary to keep track of the size of editions, or for the artist to sign impressions elsewhere than on the plate.

The introduction of lithography to France is credited to General Baron Lejeune, who actually visited Senefelder's workshop in Munich and created an image of a Cossack that won him immediate approval. In an age where people of fashion—both men and women—were frequently versed in drawing, an interest in lithography soon became *à la mode.* Among those who adopted it was the accomplished Baron Dominique Vivant Denon (1747–1825), who accompanied Napoleon to Egypt, where he made drawings for the eventual publication of his richly illustrated *Voyage in Upper and Lower Egypt* (1802). Although Denon produced several hundred lithographs, he was primarily known in his day as a diplomat and administrator. As Napoleon's director of the national museums of France, he played a conspicuous role in the founding of many of the great public museums of Europe, including the Louvre, the Prado, and the Rijksmuseum in Amsterdam. And while he did not by any means invent the fashion of "Orientalism" that enjoyed a vogue in early nineteenth-century France, Denon helped invigorate that enthusiasm.

In the flood tide of interest in lithography, numerous established masters of painting turned to that technique from time to time. Among them, Baron Antoine-Jean Gros (1771–1835) was particularly prominent. He too had accompanied Napoleon on his campaigns in the Near East, so his representations of Islamic, or "Oriental," subjects had the added cachet of reflecting authentic personal experience. Gros's *Arab of the Desert,* 1817 (fig. 1), is a fine early example of the use of lithography by a major artist of the period. Gros's well-known colleague Antoine Charles Horace Vernet, who was known as Carle Vernet (1758–1836), also tried his hand with notable success at depicting Oriental subject matter, as is vividly testified in his *Entrance to the Street of the Bazaar at Fort Joan of Arc,* of 1818 (fig. 2). Similarly, Carle Vernet's son and pupil Horace Vernet (1789–1863) also became an adept lithographer, and, while still very young, produced a notable series of prints relating to his recent service in the army. Like Gros's scenes of the Near East, younger Vernet's sympathetic scenes of French military life (fig. 3) had the added popular appeal of being based on their author's direct experience. Widely traveled and much honored, Horace Vernet returned repeatedly in his art to the exploits of the armed forces of France, throughout a long and illustrious career.

Many capable illustrators of the time similarly capitalized upon lithography as a ready vehicle for publishing military subjects, which remained popular long after Napoleon's fall, and which, in fact, served first to create, then to perpetuate the Napoleonic legend. Among them, two artists in particular are

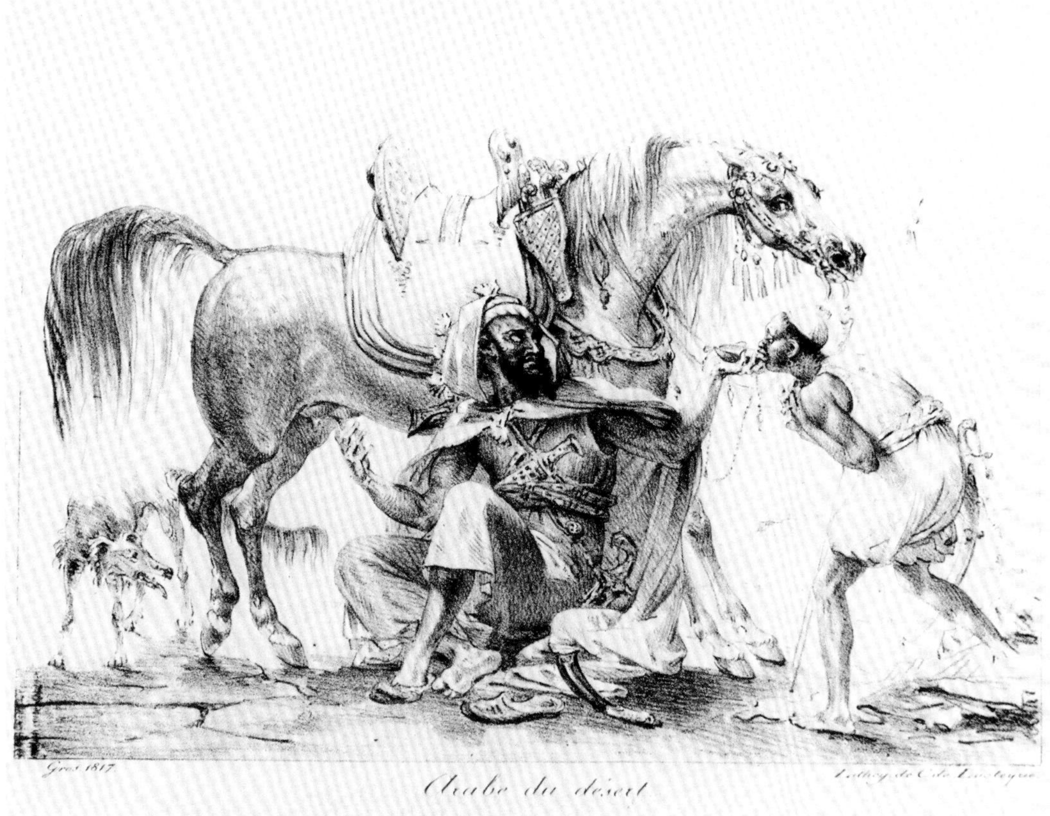



Fig. 1

Baron Antoine-Jean Gros (1771–1835)
*Arabe du desert*, 1817
Lithograph, 8 ½ x 11″
Museum purchase
1984.41

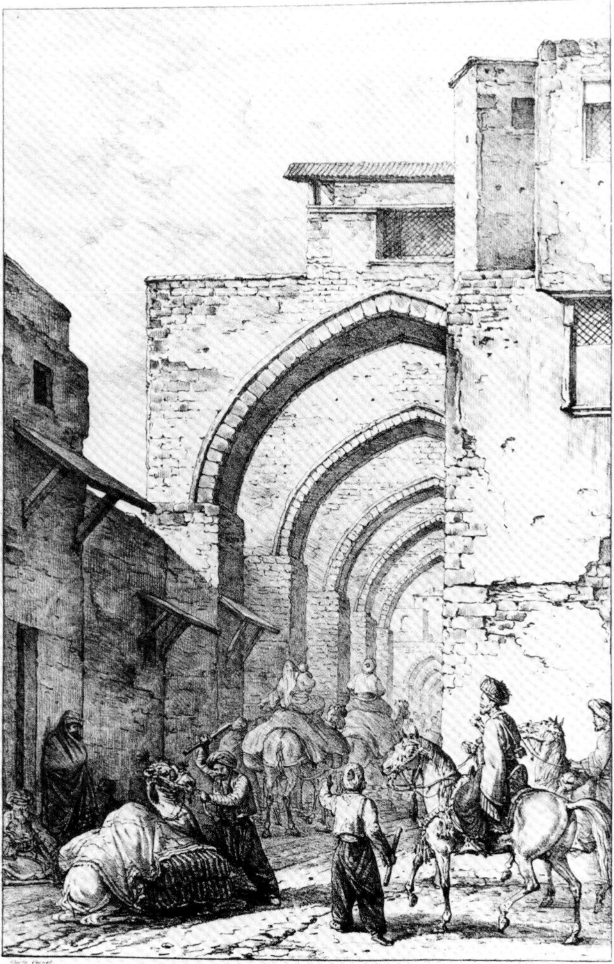

Fig. 2

Carle Vernet (1758–1836)
*Entrée de la rue du bazar à Ft. Jean d'Arc*, 1818
Lithograph, 17 x 11″
Gift of Frank Trapp
1985.39

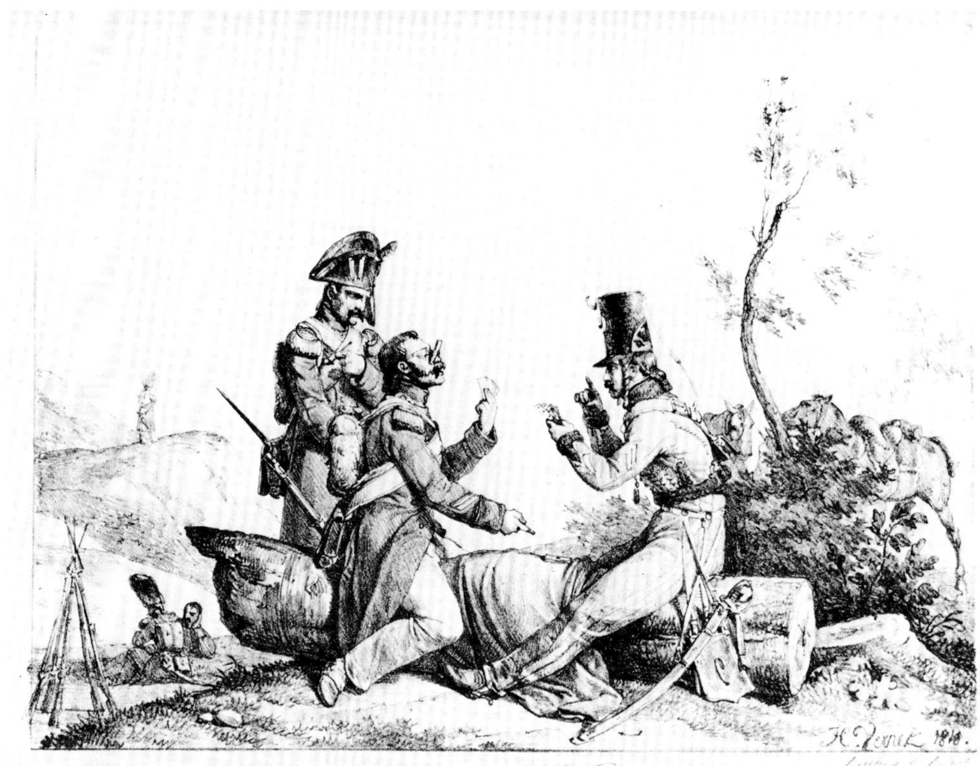



Fig. 3

Horace Vernet (1789–1863)
*Soldats jouant à la drogue,** 1818
Lithograph 7¹¹/₁₆ x 9¾″
Gift of Frank Trapp
1987.53

Fig. 4

Nicolas-Toussaint Charlet
  (1792–1845)
*L'Allocution (28 juillet 1830)*, 1830
Lithograph, 9¾ x 13″
Museum purchase
1965.37

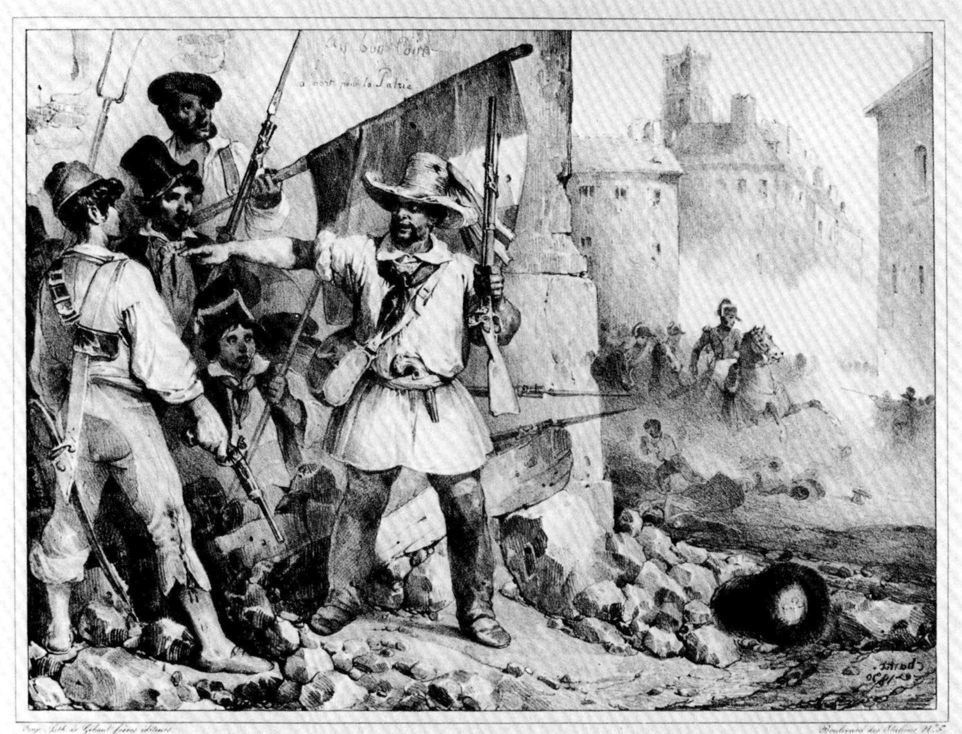



*A card game *(la drogue)* was played in
military encampments, in which the
loser had to place a forked stick on his
nose.

outstanding: Nicolas-Toussaint Charlet (1792–1845) and Auguste Raffet (1804–60). The former studied with Gros, so his interest in Napoleon came quite naturally. His illustrations for the exiled leader's diary of Saint Helena further typify his political and artistic allegiances, which were unsympathetic to the cause of the restored Bourbon dynasty (fig. 4). The somewhat younger Raffet, who studied both with Gros and Charlet, was soon deflected from his ambitions of a career in painting by his great success as a lithographer, also specializing in military illustration.

The power of the pictorial image to mold public attitudes had of course been recognized since time immemorial, and with the advent of the greater freedom of opinion in modern times, editors of various shadings of political allegiance employed artists to present their respective causes. Following the example of the British artists who had taken the lead in ridiculing public figures, a number of specialists in political caricature soon emerged in France as well. For them, the lithographic medium was made to order. That pursuit culminated in the long and towering presence of Honoré Daumier (1808–79), whose commentaries on politics and mores spanned many decades.

Daumier's genial oeuvre of over 4,000 lithographs stands by itself as a singular monument to the artist and his age. Both technically and expressively, Daumier's art evolved from the more classically defined manner of his early years of close association with the editor and political satirist Charles Philipon (1800–1862) to the ever more loosely defined and more amiably disposed glimpses of human foibles of his later years. Two examples from the print collection at Mead serve to illustrate that shift of manner and expressive tone. Daumier's retrenchment from his overt hostility toward King Louis-Philippe's new monarchy (the so-called "July Monarchy" created by the Revolution of 1830) was not wholly voluntary, however, for Daumier served a prison sentence for violating the censorship laws imposed by the government of that "burgher monarch." A sample of that hostility may be appreciated in *Celui-là, on peut le mettre en liberté! Il n'est plus dangereux* [You can free that one! He's no longer dangerous, 1834; fig. 5]. Daumier later avoided confrontations with the established regime by turning his attentions mainly to the foibles of the ordinary citizens of Paris amongst whom he lived. A sample of his unerring eye for the absurd is to be seen in one of the spoofs

Fig. 5

Honoré Daumier (1808–79)
*Celui-là, on peut le mettre en liberté!*
*Il n'est plus dangereux*, 1834
Lithograph, 8 ¾ x 10″
Museum purchase
1972.45

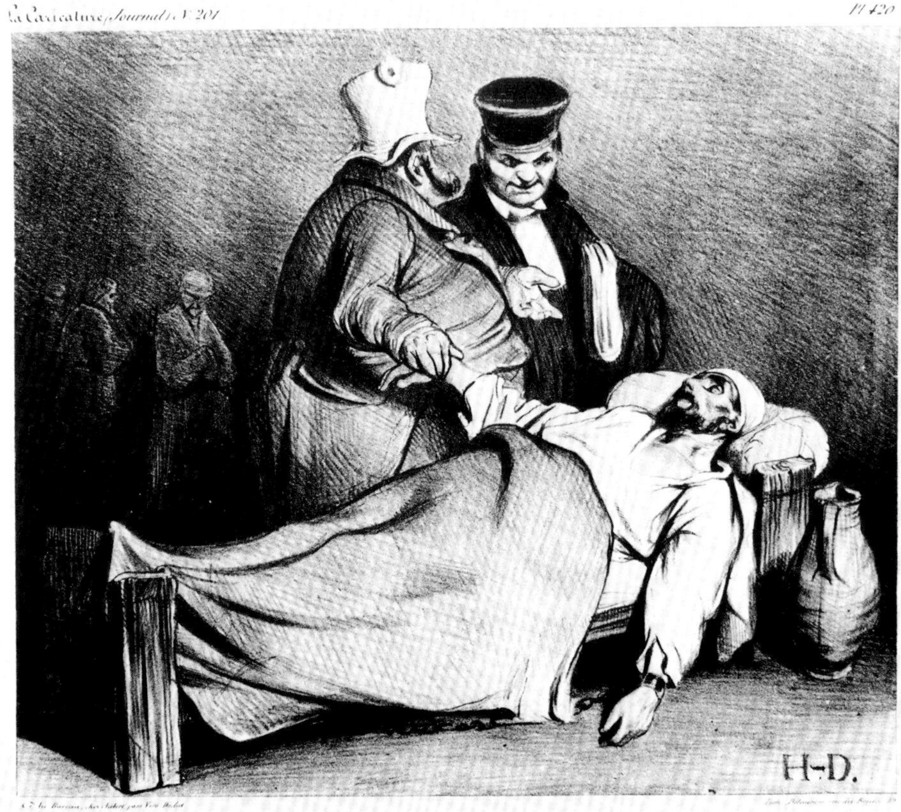

in his "Blue Stockings" series, *Oh, Moon! Inspire me this evening...* (fig. 6). Typically, the viewer here quickly senses the sympathetic warmth of the artist's own identification with the feelings of subjects whose sense of life he gently but deftly mocks.

But Daumier was only the greatest member of a distinguished company. His interest in caricature had been anticipated in other terms by Sean Grandville (1803–47). And his satire inspired numerous capable imitators. Daumier's close rivals in portrayal of the comedy of the Parisian scene included, among others, the brilliant social commentators Sulpice Guillaume Chevalier, called Paul Gavarni (1804–66), and Achille Devéria (1800–57), both of whom were also sympathetic observers of everyday life. Gavarni's lithograph *On the Road to Toulon* (fig. 7) is representative of the outstanding level of quality maintained by specialists in that appealing genre of popular lithographic illustration.

Another important group of early French lithographers remains to be noted, however, for Senefelder's new print process also kindled the interests of several artists whose reputations were mainly sustained by their accomplishments as painters. I refer to the leading spirits of the Romantic generation in France, Théodore Géricault (1791–1824) and Eugène Delacroix (1798–1863). Along with a number of contemporaries who shared their point of view, Géricault and Delacroix each produced outstanding contributions to the rich legacy of early lithography.

Where somewhat older masters like Pierre-Paul Prud'hon (1758–1823) had customarily turned over their designs to specialists for lithographic transcription, Géricault worked directly with those specialists to execute his forceful prints. As might be expected, he shared the fascination with the image of the horse that was current in the circle of his teacher, Carle Vernet, and of his closest friend and, for a time, his

Fig. 6

Honoré Daumier (1808–79)
*O Lune! Inspire-moi ce soir quelque petite un peu
    grandiose! ça je t'aime ainsi, lorsque tu me
    presentes en entier ton face pole et melancolique!
    ...mais, O Lune, je t'affectionne moins lorsque
    tu m'apparais sous la forme d'un croissant...
    parce que alors tu me rappelles tout bonnement
    mon mari!*, 1844
Lithograph, 7⅛ x 9¼″
Gift of the Wise Arts Council
1984.64h

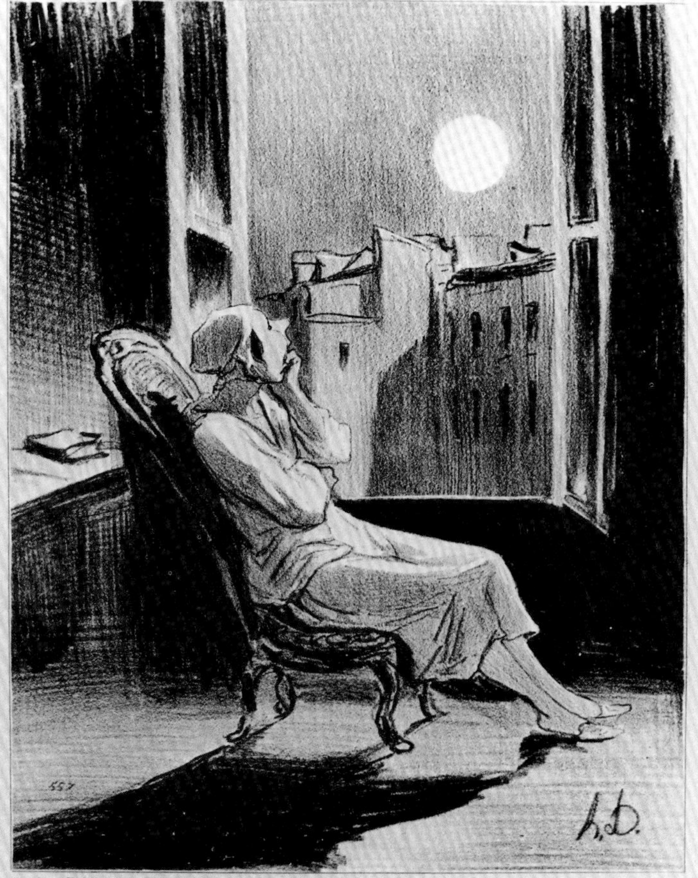

next-door neighbor, Horace Vernet. In their more Romantic emanations, as in Géricault's subjects from Lord Byron's poetry, the fiery Arab strain occurs, with the arched necks, flaring nostrils, and flowing manes and tails that Baron Gros had popularized as a virtual formula. In the last years of an all-too-brief life, Géricault became increasingly involved with the descriptive fidelity to nature that was implicit in Carle Vernet's teachings. Tendencies of the sort, which anticipate the mid-century realist doctrines of Gustave Courbet (1819–77), were intensified by Géricault's prolonged stay in England during the years 1820–22, not long before his untimely death. In that late phase of his artistic development, the powerful, weighty workhorse replaces the fleet Arabian mounts of his earlier repertory, as may be appreciated in his impressive plate *Entrance to the Adelphi Wharf*, 1821 (fig. 8).

A still more individualistic convert to lithography was that archetype of French Romanticism, Eugène

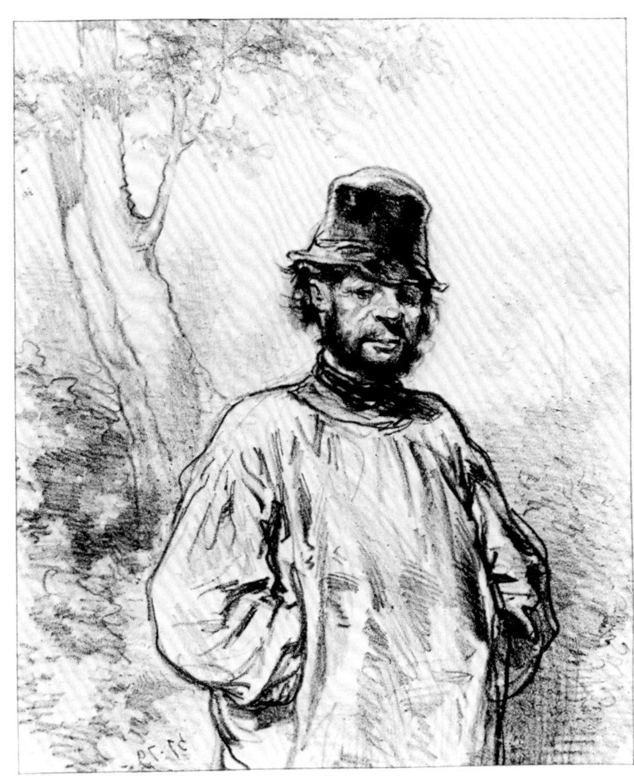

Fig. 7

Paul Gavarni (1804–66)
*Sur le chemin de Toulon*
Lithograph, 1st state of 2, 7½ x 6¼″
Museum purchase
1972.32

Jean Louis Théodore Géricault (1791–1824)
*Entrance to the Adelphi Wharf*, 1821
Lithograph, 2nd state, 12½ x 15¹³/₁₆″
Museum purchase
1965.51

Fig. 8

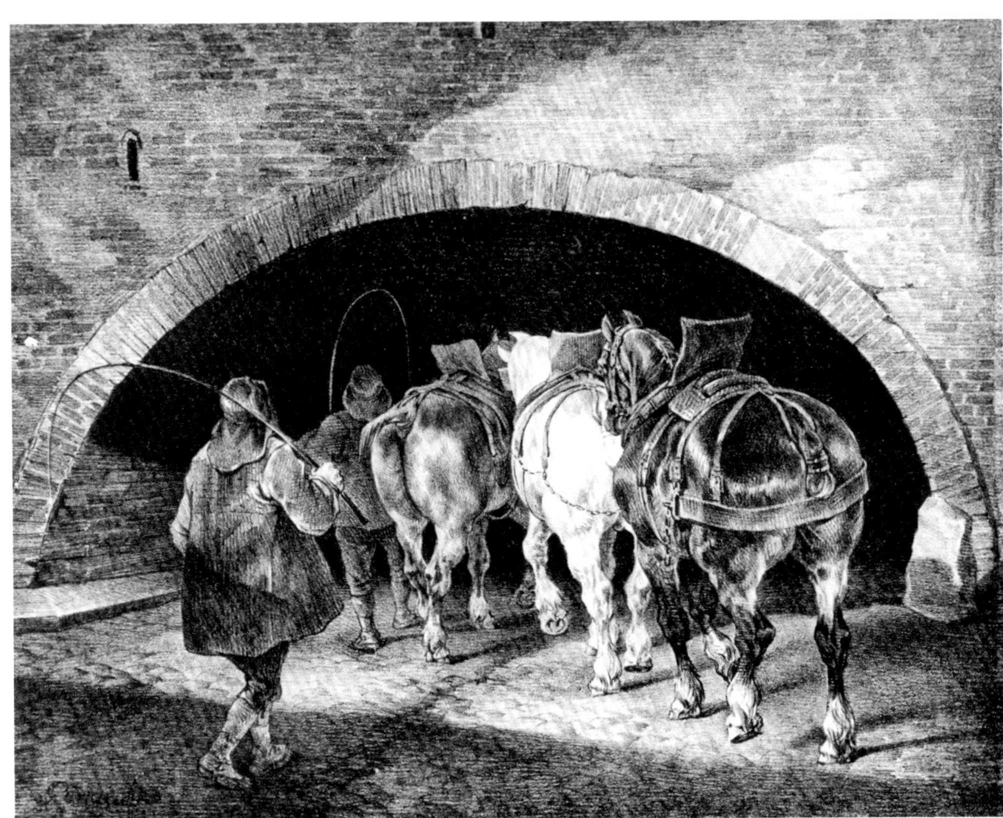

Delacroix. Although his involvements with printmaking waned in later life, Delacroix's body of prints is understandably larger than Géricault's, and it evinces a remarkable range of technical and expressive development. After producing several political caricatures that hold more interest as biographical than as strictly artistic documents, Delacroix rapidly progressed to the imposing level of mastery embodied in his *Royal Tiger* of 1829 (fig. 9). Never a patient person, however, Delacroix soon bridled at such close demands for fidelity of detail. Plates from his series of illustrations to part 1 of Goethe's *Faust* (fig. 10) show his characteristic restlessness and proneness to idiosyncrasies of style, particularly in the early state here reproduced, in which the maker's fascinating marginalia are retained. (These doodles would be eradicated in the final printing.) His excursions here into the use of *touche*, whereby the image is achieved by use of the waxy medium in liquid form, or his indulgence in the negative effects produced by scraping into dark passages, indicate Delacroix's delight in probing the resources of his chosen medium.

As his contemporaries well realized, Delacroix dominated the Romantic generation of France, once Géricault prematurely left the stage. Numerous others, however, maintained the Romantic stance with a distinction all their own. Among them the talented Louis Boulanger (1806–67) and the Johannot brothers, Alfred (1800–37) and Tony (1803–52), deserve special attention. *Royal Family*, c. 1830, by Alfred Johannot (fig. 11), serves to illustrate the high level of quality maintained among the lesser masters of Romanticism in France. But the advent of photographic processes, after the mid century, ended the fashion for lithography as a reproductive technique, in France as elsewhere. Concomitantly, a renewed interest in the etching mediums eroded interest in lithography as a vehicle for self-expression. It was not until much later in the century that the potential of lithography was explored afresh by artists of major stature, as the mere mention of Odilon Redon (1840–1916) and Henri de Toulouse-Lautrec (1864–1901) makes clear. But theirs is a different story, for by their time the remarkable period of the incunabula of lithography was already part of a fast-receding but honorable past.

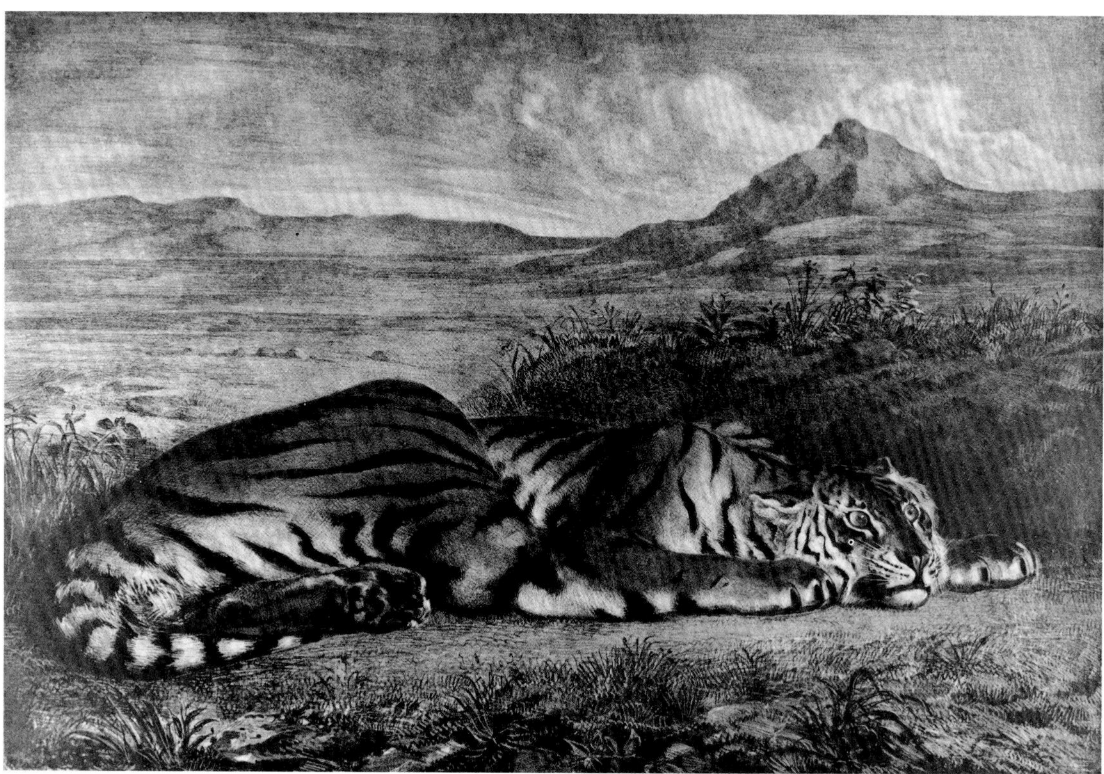

Fig. 9

Ferdinand Victor Eugène Delacroix (1798–1863)
*Tigre royal*, 1829
Lithograph, 3rd state of 4, 16 x 19¾ ″
Gift of Edward C. Crossett, '05
1951.972

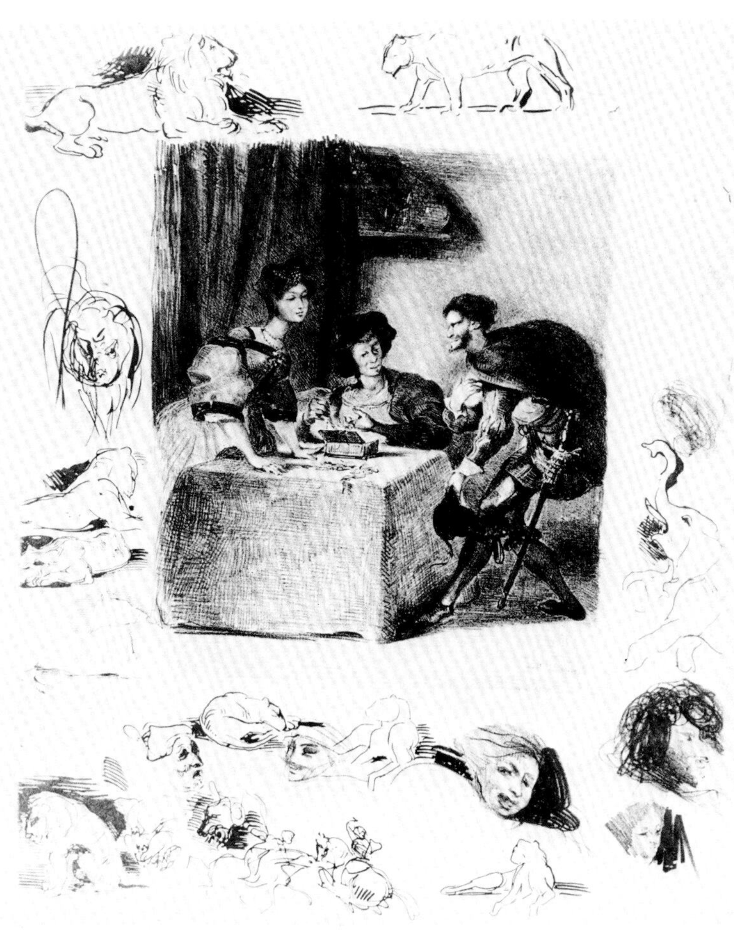

Fig. 10

Ferdinand Victor Eugène Delacroix (1798–1863)
*Mephistopheles se presente chez Marthe,*
    from ''Faust'' series, 1827
Lithograph, 1st state of 7, 16¼ x 12¾ ″
Gift of Edward C. Crossett, '05
1951.965

Fig. 11

Alfred Johannot (1800–1837)
*Le famille royale,* c. 1830
Lithograph, 7¾ x 8¼ ″
Museum purchase
1983.77

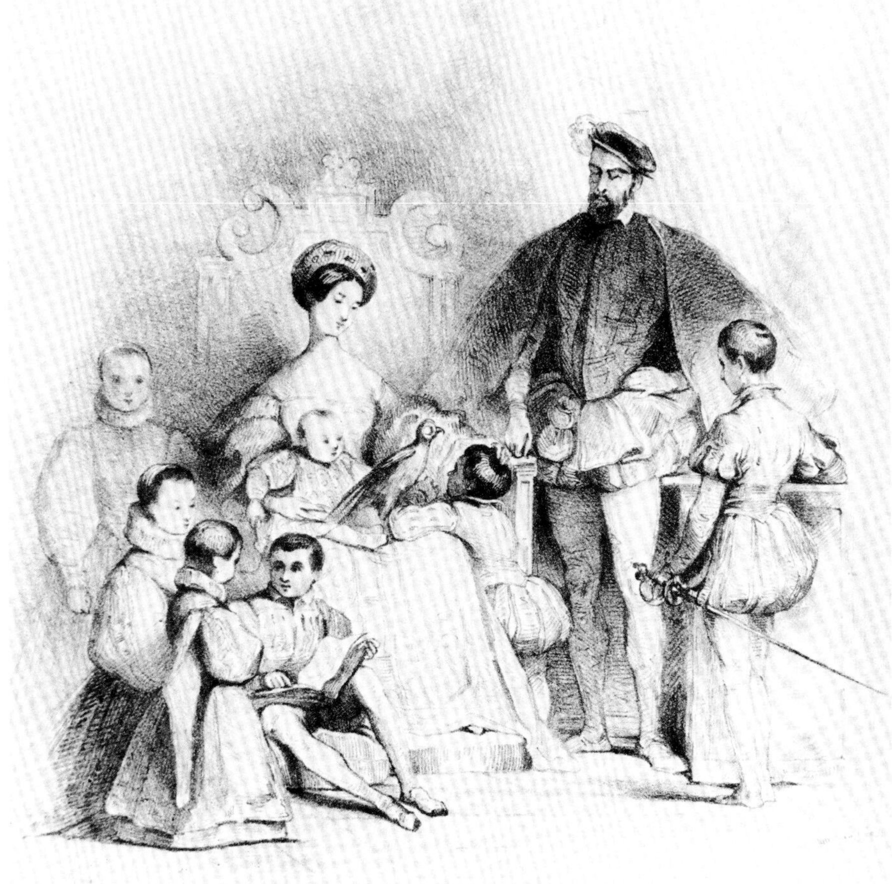

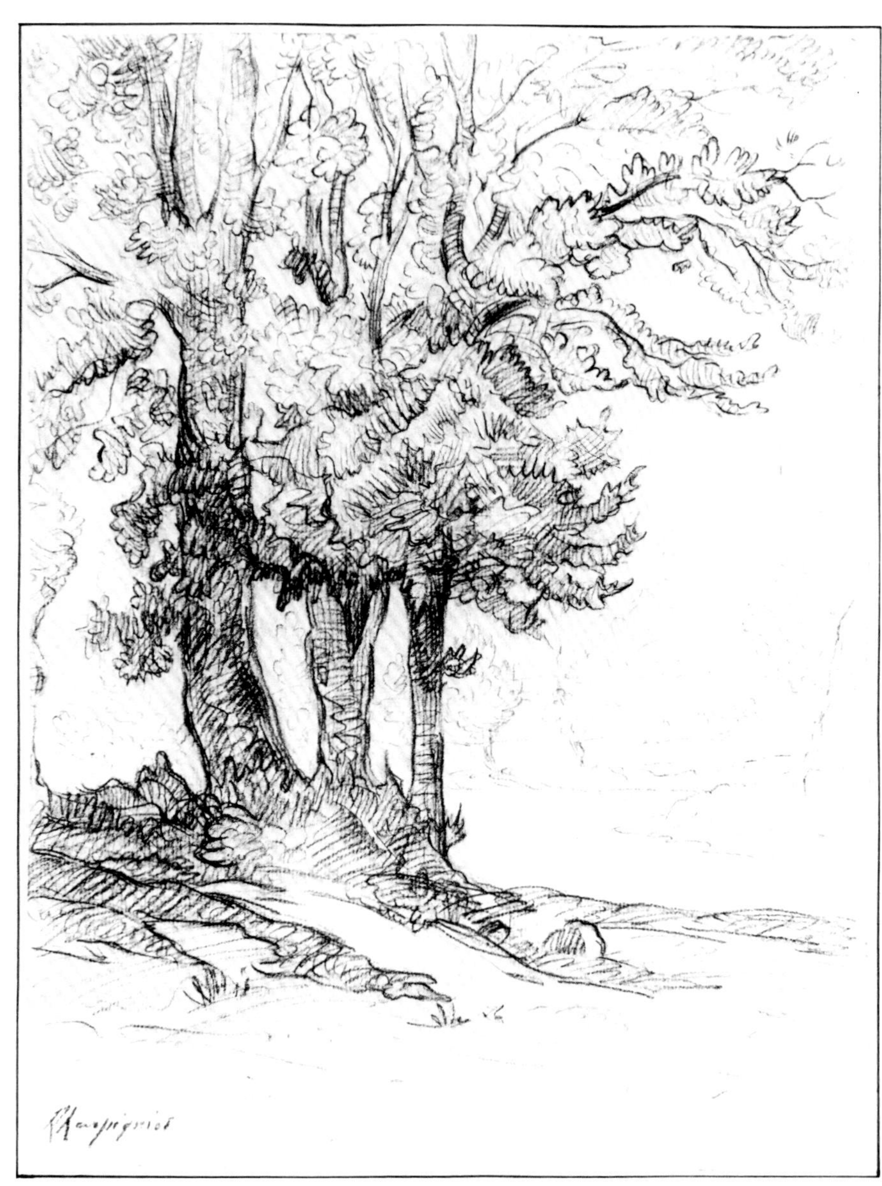

Henry Joseph Harpignies (1819–1916)
*Oak Trees*
Drawing in black crayon on light grey paper,
     17 x 12½″
Museum purchase
1948.29